LIFE
IS A
GOLD MINE
CAN YOU DIG IT?

20TH ANNIVERSARY EDITION

JOHN W. STANKO

Life is a Gold Mine: Can You Dig It?
20th Anniversary Edition
by John W. Stanko
Copyright ©2017 John W. Stanko

ISBN 978-1-63360-058-4
For Worldwide Distribution
Printed in the U.S.A.

PurposeQuest Ink
P.O. Box 8882
Pittsburgh, PA 15221-0882
412.646.2780

Table of Contents

Gold Mine Principle #5: Faith

INTRODUCTION

"How much better to get wisdom than gold, to choose understanding rather than silver!"— Proverbs 16:16.

It's hard to believe that I first wrote this book more than 20 years ago. I can still remember how exciting it was to put out my first book. When it premiered at Christian Booksellers in 1995, I was on top of the world, convinced it would become a best seller. It has done modestly well, but never reached the heights of success I had hoped and imagined. I have since learned that all first-time authors believe they will pay off their house or buy a new car with the book proceeds. Few do, and I am not among the few.

As I write, I have 28 other books along with several revisions and rewrites. This is the third version of *Life is a Gold Mine*, and this time, I have made some major changes that I will explain later. While my material has expanded and hopefully matured, I am still called upon to teach and coach people concerning the topics in this book. I am more convinced than ever that these concepts are part of the foundation for a successful and meaningful life, and I plan on teaching them until I have no strength left to do so. Who knows, maybe another revision is down the road before I go on to my eternal resting place.

Life Is a Gold Mine was born during a time of great personal frustration. In 1985 I was administrator and ministry coordinator for a large local church, and I wasn't happy. There was so much to do in the church, and from my viewpoint, not enough people involved. As we would finish a project, someone would invariably approach me and say something like, "I'm sorry

I wasn't involved. I felt the Lord prompting me to do something and offer to help, and I like to do what you were doing, but I was afraid and didn't know anyone, so I didn't volunteer."

Without fail, the person had the skills, gifts, and training that we needed. But even after repeated announcements during church services and inquiries to pastors and leaders, people were still uninvolved.

There were others who expressed to me their desire to be in "full-time ministry." Often employed in significant and well-paying secular jobs, they were discouraged that they weren't in any kind of "ministry." Some actually left those positions and today are still wandering, trying to find how they can best serve the Lord.

Richard Nelson Bolles described this dilemma in his book, *What Color Is Your Parachute?*:

> We want some guidance and help in this area, because we want to marry our religious beliefs with our work, rather than leaving the two—our religion and our work—compartmentalized, as two areas of our life which never talk to each other. We want them to talk to each other and uplift each other.[1]

I began asking the Lord, "How can I help people de-compartmentalize their lives? How can I find volunteers? Better yet, how can I help people find out what they are born to do, and help them do it? How can I help them see that full-time ministry is not the only way to serve the Lord? How can I convince them that if they're doing what You have called them to do—and using their gifts in the process—they are serving You?"

During this time, our church had a sendoff for a pastoral staff member. As we were praying for this man and his family, a prophetic word came that changed my life. It was an answer to the questions I had been asking and contained the reasons why so few were involved and so many were unfulfilled. It also contained the remedy for the problem I was facing. Here is part of that prophetic message:

> In many countries where there is poverty, it is not because there are not resources. In many nations where people go hungry, it is not because the soil is poor. Where they lack industrial development, it is not because there are not minerals in the ground. It is because the people haven't discovered and learned to use what they have. And because the minerals lie in the earth, and the soil—rich as it is—lies dormant, there is poverty abounding in the land. But when someone comes along who knows what to look for and where to find it and how to use it, there are jobs, and there is productivity, and there is wealth. And some sit in their poverty and say it is unfair that we should be poor and others should be rich, but it is not unfair. It is ignorance. It is not knowing what is beneath their feet and what is around them and what is theirs to use.
>
> So it is in the church of the Lord Jesus Christ. In some parts there is great wealth; there is great growth; there is great power. In other parts there is great drought. There is spiritual starvation, and people perish for want of the Word of God; perish for lack of the Spirit of God; perish for lack of edification. They perish and wane away in their spirits. It is not because the resources are not there, because within them, within those very people, within those very congregations, lie great riches, great promises and great wealth. The need is to discover what is there and use it and appropriate it and get it out so that it can become productive.

When I heard this, I almost jumped out of my chair! First, this told me that the resources were out there. The right people for every job were there. The Holy Spirit had gifted and called each one. There was no lack of people, but there was a lack of knowledge about how to find and motivate them to become productive.

The second thing this told me was that someone needed to help discover and channel the human resources in every church. If someone could call forth the people and the deposit of the Holy Spirit in them, then the body of Christ would become stronger and more effective.

And finally, it let me know that each person had a purpose and gifts that were from the Holy Spirit. It was up to the Spirit as to where and how these resources would be fulfilled and used, and not all of them would find their expression in the Church.

From that day, I set out to develop a seminar and write a book to help people become more productive and fulfilled in their life's purpose. I wanted people to know that they were born to do what they were doing. If their purpose was auto mechanics, they needed the assurance that they were serving and worshiping God with each engine tuneup.

From there, I wanted to set people on a course of action that would refine and release those resources. It was in my heart to help every man and woman get out of the grandstands and into the game. I wanted to challenge them to dig for the true riches in their life. *Life Is a Gold Mine: Can You Dig It?* was born.

I chose gold and digging as symbols of what I was after for several reasons. The book of Proverbs says, "My [wisdom] fruit is better than gold, yes, than fine gold and my revenue than choice silver" (Proverbs 8:19 NKJV). In fact, the Bible is full of comparisons of spiritual things to gold. For instance:

- "The law from your mouth is more precious to me than thousands of pieces of silver and gold" (Psalm 119:72).

- The ordinances of the Lord are sure and altogether righteous. They are more precious than gold (Psalm 19:9-10).

- These have come so that your faith—of greater worth than gold, which perishes even though refined by fire—may be proved genuine (1 Peter 1:7).

Gold is indeed one of the most precious metals known to man. Yet the Word of God, your faith, and the wisdom and understanding that come from knowing your purpose are more valuable than gold. As I researched the mineral gold, I discovered several characteristics that made it the correct focus for what I wanted to teach.

First, gold is found alongside many other minerals, and traces of it are even found in sea water. That's how it is with God's mission for our lives. It is often expressed as we carry out some of the more common aspects of life. We can look at ourselves and what we're doing and not see the riches that are buried there. A little digging, however, reveals what is there and begins the recovery process.

Second, once gold ore is mined, the gold is then easily recovered in the refining process. It's the same with our spiritual resources: a little "refining" and we can shine forth like a nugget of pure gold.

Third was something that I already knew: Gold is attractive in color and brightness. When we function in our God-given purpose, with power and creativity, we're also attractive and exciting to be around.

Finally, gold is durable and malleable. It can endure all kinds of treatment and be shaped into many forms. Purpose is like that. Even after the dealings of God and men, you are still able to function in many different kinds of life and ministry situations.

As I've taught this seminar all over the country, I've found most people are hungry, even desperate, to know what their purpose is and how they can fulfill it. No one wants to lead a wasted life. You want to be like Paul who, at the end of his life, said: "I have finished the race, I have kept the faith" (2 Timothy 4:7). To say that, you must know what the race is so you can know when you've finished. You must know what the course is if Jesus is ever to say to you, "Well done, good and faithful servant" (Matthew 25:21).

Mining and refining, however, are hard work. With all the above being true, if you're not willing to dig out your gold, you'll have only the potential for riches. The gold is there, but you can die with it still buried in the recesses of your life. Knowing that the gold is there, the question is, "Can you dig it?" I hope this book will help you do just that. As we "dig," I have included some "gold nuggets" from the book of Proverbs for your consideration.

In my first two editions, I spent a great deal of time referencing Stephen Covey's classic book, *The 7 Habits of Highly Effective People*. I did this for several reasons. One was that Covey's book was widely popular when I first wrote in 1995. Also, Covey's worldview differed from mine, so I wanted to make some points that I felt Covey missed or misinterpreted. Looking back, I was hoping to "cash in" on his popularity. I wanted to read a book review that said something like this: "John Stanko, in his new book, builds on what Stephen Covey had to say and shares with us important insights that the *7 Habits* missed."

Well, Covey sold millions of copies of his book, and I sold thousands. So much for piggybacking on the success of someone else! Yet there was another important reason that I chose to include Covey, because in 1995 I was not confident I had anything to say that people would really want to hear or read. I thought if I included Covey, it would enhance my own credibility.

In fact, I had to face the fact that several of my early books were not really books, they were book reports about other people's books. I have since come to realize that this was all rooted in fear: fear that I had nothing to say, fear that what I had to say others would not agree with, that I needed to use other people's names because my name was not enough.

Even my early use of social media in 2005 revealed this fear. I would often include daily quotes from other authors and famous leaders with my "friends" on Facebook and Twitter.

Every once in a while, I would include something from my own work—but not often. When I did, people would respond positively, some writing to say that they looked forward to my "stankoisms" more than the quotes from others.

Finally, I began to "mine" my own writings and creativity to send out daily devotionals, quotes, and sayings (all within Twitter's 140-character limit). I stopped quoting others so often in my books and began to have confidence that my insight in my own words had merit. The feedback from readers and listeners told me that assumption was correct. I wrote all that to write this: Mr. Covey will not be as prominently featured in this 20th anniversary edition—but he will still be included from time to time.

Also, I have made some major adjustments to the content and focus of the book's material that I think will make it more readable and helpful. Here is a summary of the three major changes you can expect:

> 1. I now call the principles discussed in this book the Gold Mine Principles. I never used that term in the first two editions.
>
> 2. The Principles in the first two books were purpose, goal setting, time management, organization, and faith. In this updated version, I have combined two of the original Principles and have added a new Principle. Now the five Principles include: 1) purpose; 2) creativity; 3) goal setting; 4) time management; and 5) faith.
>
> 3. There are many new examples and teaching perspectives that make the Principles easier to understand and apply.

Since I released the first edition of *Life is a Gold Mine* in 1995, I have spoken in 42 countries, written several dozen books, started my company called PurposeQuest, launched my purposequest.com website, established Kenya PurposeQuest, relocated back to my home city of Pittsburgh, and met and coached thousands of people all over the world. My conclusion after all that is the Gold Mine Principles have never been more important if you are interested in living a meaningful and productive life. Twenty years after I introduced them in this book and in my seminars, I am still studying and learning how to apply them in my life and equip others to do the same.

I want you to know the joy I've known as I've functioned in my life's purpose. I want you to preach, teach, pilot a plane, sew a dress, repair brakes, or serve your boss knowing that you're hitting the mark and functioning in what you were born to do. Wouldn't it be wonderful to know that what you do five, six, or seven days a week is as worshipful as standing in the pew and singing? Those who function in their purpose fulfill Paul's exhortation in Romans 12:1: "Offer your bodies as living sacrifices, holy and pleasing to God—this is your spiritual act of worship."

Bolles wrote in *What Color is Your Parachute?*:

> Every keen observer of human nature will know what I mean when I say that those who have found some sense of Mission have a very special joy, "which no one can take from them." It is wonderful to feel that beyond eating, sleeping, working, having pleasure and it may be marrying, having children, and growing older, you were set here on Earth for some special purpose, and that you can gain some idea of what that purpose is.

Bolles then presents "a scenario for the romantic" of how it is that we come to know or rediscover our purpose:

> We may imagine that before we came to Earth, our souls, our Breath, our Light, stood before the great Creator and volunteered for this Mission. And God and we, together, chose what that Mission would be and what particular gifts would be needed, which he then agreed to give us, after our birth. Thus, our Mission was not a command given peremptorily by an unloving Creator to a reluctant slave without a vote, but was a task jointly designed by us both,

in which as fast as the great Creator said, "I wish" our hearts responded, "Oh, yes." As mentioned in an earlier Comment, it may be helpful to think of the condition of our becoming human as that we became amnesiac about any consciousness our soul had before birth—and therefore amnesiac about the nature or manner in which our Mission was designed. Our searching for our Mission now is therefore a searching to recover the memory of something we ourselves had a part in designing. I am admittedly a hopeless romantic, so of course I like this picture.[2]

I have given you some steps to follow at the end of each section to apply what you've learned as you seek to recover from your amnesia, but I've kept them basic. My purpose in writing is to see you fulfill your life's mission as you carry out your daily responsibilities as a student, wife, father, employee, supervisor, or minister. As a church leader, I want to equip you so that you can work effectively. As an administrator, I want to help you do things efficiently. It's from those motives that I write, and it's in that spirit that I hope you receive this work. Your life is indeed a gold mine. Now let's get on with the digging.

GOLD MINE PRINCIPLE #1

PURPOSE

Staking Your Claim

*"He who works his land will have abundant food,
but the one who chases fantasies will have his
fill of poverty."*—Proverbs 28:19

Chapter 1
An Overview

Let's start by looking at Acts 6:1-7:

> In those days when the number of the disciples was increasing, the Grecian Jews among them complained against the Hebraic Jews because their widows were being overlooked in the daily distribution of food. So the Twelve gathered all the disciples together and said, "It would not be right for us to neglect the ministry of the word of God in order to wait on tables. Brothers, choose seven men from among you who are known to be full of the Spirit and wisdom. We will turn this responsibility over to them, and will give our attention to prayer and the ministry of the word." This proposal pleased the whole group. They chose Stephen, a man full of faith and of the Holy Spirit; also Philip, Procorus, Nicanor, Timon, Parmenas, and Nicolas from Antioch, a convert to Judaism. They presented these men to the apostles, who prayed and laid their hands on them. So the word of God spread. The number of disciples in Jerusalem increased rapidly, and a large number of priests became obedient to the faith.

The Bible never hides the human weaknesses of those who served the Lord. In Acts 6, we have an account of a serious problem in the church. The Hebrew and Greek believers were fussing at one another. There was an oversight in care that was at least cultural and at worst ethnic. There was also inefficiency.

People were upset, talking, and complaining about the problem. It sounds like life in many churches and organizations today.

It's important to study and understand how the apostles handled this problem. Five principles in these verses will form the basis for this book and I have come to identify them as the Gold Mine Principles. The first Principle is **purpose**, which I referred to as effectiveness when I first began to teach the Principles. Effectiveness is both knowing your purpose and functioning in it. *Vine's Dictionary of Old and New Testament Words* defines effectiveness as being "full of power to achieve results." The apostles were well aware of what God wanted them to do. You, too, have a purpose in life that can also be identified. God wants you to know what it is. Your success depends on how closely you stick to activities that express your purpose.

The second Principle is implied in the Acts 6 passage, and that is the Principle of **creativity**. The apostles faced a problem that no one had ever faced before. They had to come up with a solution that would be true to their values of helping the widows while staying true to their purpose. Therefore, they created a position today referred to as a deacon and these men were assigned the responsibility of caring for the widows.

Verse four contains the third Principle, **goal setting**. The apostles set a high goal of devoting themselves to prayer and the Word without distraction. They probably had goals of how long to pray, what to study, and how they would carry the Gospel to the nations. It's likewise important for you to set lofty goals for your job, family, ministry, and personal life; you'll learn how to do this in Section Three.

This leads to a fourth Principle, **time management**. The apostles realized a great harvest of people because they were efficient in their use of time. They knew their priorities in life, and devoted time to carrying out those priorities on a daily basis. Formerly, organization was the fourth Principle, but we will cover that in the section on time, for if you are organized where your time is concerned, you will tend to be organized in other areas, like your computer files, desktop or work area, and financial matters.

The fifth and final Principle is **faith**. The apostles had faith in God and the people. They trusted that the people would choose the right men, and they trusted that the Lord would help these men carry out this important job.

When the apostles applied the Gold Mine Principles, the church functioned properly. Those who ministered to the widows did so in the power of the Holy Spirit. Those who gave themselves to the Word and prayer did so with excellence. The number of disciples increased greatly, and the whole process flowed smoothly. As they walked in faith, the apostles created an organization that was remarkable for its effectiveness, excellence, and efficiency.

In this first Section, let's look more closely at the first Principle, which is finding and fulfilling your life purpose.

Chapter 2
Waiting on Tables

As we saw in the previous chapter, the apostles in Acts 6 had a problem to solve. There was both good news and bad news in the Church, the plot of ground that God had given them to work: "He who works his land will have abundant food, but the one who chases fantasies will have his fill of poverty" (Proverbs 28:19).

The good news was that the number of disciples was increasing. The word of the Lord was spreading rapidly and many were making decisions to follow Jesus. These conversions generated a lot of activity and ministry needs. The apostles, hand-picked and trained by the Lord Himself, were the natural choices to train and direct the growth of these early disciples. Due to this explosive growth, however, they found themselves totally immersed in the life of this emerging body of believers.

Now for the bad news: Some of the widows were being overlooked in the daily distribution of food. The Grecian Jews (their main language was Greek rather than Aramaic, and they lived is separate sections of Jerusalem), whose widows were not being taken care of, approached these leaders and apostles for help. That led to more bad news, for the apostles had their hands full seeking God for direction on how to lead the new converts and continue to promote church growth. The Grecian Jews wanted action and probably expected these leaders to personally oversee the solution. What were the apostles to do?

Covey wrote in *The 7 Habits of Highly Effective People*:

It's incredibly easy to get caught up in an activity trap, in the busyness of life, to work harder and harder at climbing the ladder of success only to discover it's leaning against the wrong wall. It is possible to be busy—very busy—without being very effective... How different our lives are when we really know what is deeply important to us, and, keeping that picture in mind, we manage ourselves each day to be and to do what really matters most. If the ladder is not leaning against the right wall, every step we take just gets us to the wrong place faster. We may be very busy, we may be very efficient, but we will also be truly effective only when we begin with the end in mind.[1]

For Covey, the "end in mind" was determining what you want to be known for and then preparing to actually do that very thing. The apostles in Acts 6 had the "end in mind" and decided they could not "wait on tables." Their purpose was not to minister to the widows (waiting on tables) but rather to devote themselves to the word of God and prayer. They could have climbed the ladder of their ministry by serving the widows only to find it leaning against the wrong wall. The right spot for the apostles was the place on the wall marked "the word of God and prayer."

This section on purpose is subtitled, "Know Where to Stake Your Claim." If the early gold miners were to find gold, it was critical that they worked the proper piece of ground. Once they found the right field, they had to stake a claim to show that the field was theirs. Otherwise, they would lose all that they had gained from their sacrifices. You also need to stake your claim carefully and then work the land that is part of your claim. You will find real gold only by giving yourself to the purpose God has assigned you—that is your field.

When verse four says that the apostles gave themselves to "prayer and the ministry of the Word," it doesn't refer to the normal devotional life that every believer is expected to maintain. Certainly all the early believers were taught to pray and study the Scriptures. The apostles, however, had a unique role to play in the Word and prayer. They had been with Jesus, and things they saw and were taught made them vital to the future of the covenant community. They knew their purpose and said, "We can't get involved in this because we have to give ourselves to something else." Waiting on tables would have taken them away from that purpose.

Your purpose gives new meaning to the verse found in Ephesians 2:10: "For we are God's handiwork, created in Christ Jesus to do good works, which God prepared in advance for us to do." The good works referred to in this verse are not just random acts of kindness that you are to perform. The good works are those things that only you can produce because you are uniquely gifted, skilled, and called to do those works. For me, writing is one of those "good works." I write quickly and I have been told I write clearly. That is because God is with me when I write. He is not with me in the same way when I sing, because that is not connected to my purpose.

When the apostles prayed, buildings shook (see Acts 4:23-31). When they gave their attention to prayer and the ministry of the Word, thousands came to the Lord (see Acts 2:40-41). If you can do something and shake a building or see significant results, you need to be doing that as often as possible. God wants you to know what your purpose is, and He will confirm it by the results you get.

Gold Nugget #1

"Let your eyes look straight ahead, fix your gaze directly before you. Make level paths for your feet and take only ways that are firm. Do not swerve to the right or the left."
—Proverbs 4:25-27

You need this same mentality as the apostles had, whether you're in the ministry or serving the Lord in some other area. You may be doing good things, even biblical things, but are you giving yourself to the thing that God has set aside for you to do?

8

Have you staked your spiritual claim in the right field? If not, you need to say, like the apostles, "I can't do that. For me, that is waiting on tables." While revising this book, I've had to say no to other things, because this is what God has put before me. Anything else at this time would be "waiting on tables" for me.

You may have a good job that has given you a high standard of living, but perhaps you feel trapped and unfulfilled. If you're staying in that job because of the money, the Bible has a name for you and it's a hireling! If you're shuffling papers, when you really feel your purpose is to start a business, counsel, create artistic works, repair, or teach, then you are "waiting on tables" even if you're paid handsomely to do what you are presently doing.

Here's another example of what I mean. I have to be honest— as a pastor I didn't like hospital visitation. I used to jokingly tell the people I pastored, "If you want mercy, don't come to me. That's not my gift." I didn't mind going to see someone who was in my congregation. But when someone wanted me to visit the cousin of their aunt by marriage whom I had never met before, I started to think of all the things I could possibly be doing so that I could honestly say, "I'm busy."

I realize that as a disciple and brother I must develop mercy and compassion for others, but some of the expectations that people had for me as a pastor constituted "waiting on tables." They had an idea of what a pastor should be and wanted me to fit their ideal.

You may think I'm unspiritual or wasn't really cut out to be a pastor because I didn't like hospital visitation. I don't see it like that at all. I preferred to find a team of people who felt called to hospital ministry, from whom the gifts of mercy, faith, and intercession flow. It seemed wise to me to identify and release those whose purpose it was to extend mercy and then let them do what they did best They would be fulfilling their purpose— in the process, they would free me up to fulfill mine.

Peter Drucker, in his book, *The Effective Executive*, has a chapter entitled, "What Can I Contribute?" In so many words, he urges everyone in an organization to focus on what he or she is capable of contributing:

> The effective executive focuses on contribution.... The focus on contribution is the key to effectiveness: in a man's own work—its content, its level, its standards, and its impacts; in his relations with others—his superiors, his associates, his subordinates; in his use of the tools of the executive such as meetings or reports.... To focus on contribution is to focus on effectiveness.[2]

Your best contribution to and role in any organization is what you're gifted and divinely enabled to do, and that relates to your purpose.

Saying no to activities or projects can be difficult (and often not possible if your supervisor asks you to do something), but it's more difficult to continually function in something that's not your purpose. It's so easy, especially in the ministry, to get caught up in other people's expectations—the purpose *they* think you should have.

Can you picture the widows on the way to the meeting described in Acts 6? Perhaps they were talking on the way saying, "Peter is my favorite apostle. I love him so much. Peter will help me." Another widow was saying, "No, John is tops in my book. He's a dear, and I know that he'll do something." You can be sure that Peter and John responded to those widows, "We're sorry, but we can't help you because it will take us away from our purpose. However, we'll find someone else who can meet your needs."

A number of years ago, a movie called *Chariots of Fire* told the story of Eric Liddel, an Olympic runner, missionary to China, and eventual martyr. At one point in the film, Liddel's sister expressed concern that he was devoting too much time to running. She was afraid it would take him away from his call as a missionary.

Liddel's response, while perhaps fictional, is still a classic. He told her that God made him fast, "And when I run," he said, "I feel His pleasure." What do you do that releases God's pleasure? Isn't that what you want to do as often as possible?

As stated earlier, God wants you to know your purpose. One of the indicators of your purpose is that you get results. Another is that you have a sense of joy and fulfillment when you do things related to your purpose. Joy is God's indicator He has placed inside you so that you will know when you are on the right track where purpose is concerned.

When I plan conferences, I feel God's pleasure. The Holy Spirit always helps me when I plan them; and time and again, God has covered my conference mistakes by His grace. I know His anointing will show up because conferences are part of my purpose (which I will describe in Chapter Four). When I "step to the plate" at a conference, I expect to hit a "home run." When I go to the hospital, on the other hand, I'm happy just to get to first base.

The heroes of the Bible knew their purpose and concentrated on fulfilling it. That's why they were so successful. Let's turn now to a quick study of purpose in God's Word.

Chapter 3

God's Presence Reveals His Purpose

God is a God of purpose. I challenge you to find one person in the Bible to whom God appeared without revealing His purpose, for God's presence and purpose go hand in hand. The presence of God isn't just a place to get goose bumps. Too many believers, I'm afraid, just want to go from spiritual high to high. When they can't find that high, they bounce from church to church. But my spiritual "high," if I may call it that, always comes from doing, at any given time, what I know I was born to do.

It's true that you will sometimes feel His presence, but that's not the end God has in mind. God's presence comes to change you and to help you better understand who He is and what He wants you to do.

Gold Nugget #2

"The Lord has made everything for its own purpose, even the wicked for the day of evil."
—Proverbs 16:4 (NAS)

Let's examine some biblical examples. The Lord told Adam that his purpose was to "be fruitful and increase in number; fill the earth and subdue it" (Genesis 1:28); Eve was to be "a helper suitable" (Genesis 2:18) for Adam; Abraham was to be a great nation and a blessing to all the peoples of the earth (Genesis 12:2-3); Joseph's purpose was to rule over his father's sons (Genesis 37:8); Moses was "to bring my people the Israelites out of Egypt" (Exodus 3:10); the nation of Israel was to be the Lord's treasured possession, "a kingdom of priests and a holy nation" (Exodus 19:5-6); even Pharaoh, a pagan ruler, fulfilled God's purpose, for Exodus 9:16 says, "I have raised you [Pharaoh] up for this very purpose, that I might show you my power and that my name might be proclaimed in all the earth."

There are many more examples of God's presence and purpose acting as one. Joshua was to lead the people to inherit the promised land (Joshua 1:6); David was to be king of Israel (1 Samuel 16:12-13); Isaiah was to "go and tell this people" (Isaiah 6:9); Jeremiah, from before the womb, was appointed "as a prophet to the nations" (Jeremiah 1:5); and Esther was made queen to save her people from destruction, as her cousin Mordecai reminded her when he said, "Who knows but that you have come to royal position for such a time as this?" (Esther 4:14). It's of note that not all of these people were in "religious" work. The Lord called some to function in secular positions (such as Esther, Joseph, and David).

We can also see God's calling and purpose in the New Testament. John the Baptist came to "prepare the way for the Lord, make straight paths for him" (Matthew 3:3). His purpose was so clear to him that, when the people declared him to be the Messiah, he insisted that he was not. John knew what his purpose was and could not be diverted. Peter and Andrew were to be "fishers of men" (Matthew 4:19). Peter was also given "the keys of the kingdom of heaven" (Matthew 16:19), so you could say his purpose was to be heaven's doorkeeper!

Acts 13:36 says, "For when David had served God's *purpose* in his own generation, he fell asleep" (emphasis added). I can't find any place in the Old or New Testaments where God didn't reveal purpose when He made His presence known to someone. It's my prayer that, like David, I too will serve God's purpose in my generation. When I go to my eternal rest, I want to say like Paul, "I have finished the race, I have kept the faith" (2

Timothy 4:7). Like Paul, I want to know my course and know that I ran it well.

If God has called me to wait on tables (and it was the purpose for some in Acts 6), then I want to wait on tables so that the angels will marvel. But if tables are not my purpose, I want to avoid them like I would a disease. How far can we take this concept? Let's take a look at John 17:1-5.

> Father, the time has come. Glorify your Son, that your Son may glorify you. For you granted him authority over all people that he might give eternal life to all those you have given him. Now this is eternal life: that they may know you, the only true God, and Jesus Christ, whom you have sent. *I have brought you glory on earth by completing the work you gave me to do.* And now, Father, glorify me in your presence with the glory I had with you before the world began (emphasis added).

Jesus brought glory to the Father by doing the work He was sent to do. He didn't glorify God by singing and praising or by being doctrinally correct. He brought glory to God by being faithful to the purpose assigned Him by the Father. You'll glorify God in the same manner as you pursue and complete the work that has been set aside for you and you alone.

One day Jesus went to Jericho and found himself in the midst of a procession. A short man climbed up a tree to get a better look at what was going on. When Jesus passed by, He said, "Zacchaeus, come down immediately. I must stay at your house today" (Luke 19:5). Zacchaeus obeyed and welcomed Him with a dinner. After dinner, Zacchaeus stood and announced, "Look, Lord! Here and now I give half of my possessions to the poor, and if I have cheated anybody out of anything, I will pay back four times the amount" (Luke 19:8).

Imagine the shock among the people, especially his fellow tax collectors. But Jesus responded, "Today salvation has come to this house, because this man, too, is a son of Abraham. For the Son of Man came *to seek and to save what was lost*" (Luke

19:9-10, emphasis added). Jesus' purpose was summarized in that simple statement. The people tried to make Him a king, a political deliverer, and a rabbi. Yet He resisted all those titles and roles because they weren't consistent with His purpose. When He ran to the lost, so to speak, He felt God's pleasure. He understood this, and told the Pharisees, "I have not come to call the righteous, but sinners" (Matthew 9:13).

It can be argued that Jesus came to fully understand and fulfill His purpose the same way you will realize yours—by seeking God. As a 12-year-old, Jesus was in the Temple seeking His purpose. He had to be about His Father's business, but first He had to know what that business was. Was it to ride into Jerusalem on a white stallion as a general? To restore Israel politically as a world power? To show forth the Father's power by great miracles and public displays?

Jesus found His purpose and focused on it the same way you will find and carry out yours. He set His face like flint to find it and then He did it. Hebrews 12:2 says, "For the joy set before him, He endured the cross, scorning its shame, and sat down at the right hand of the throne of God." For the joy of the purpose that was assigned to Him, He went through all kinds of grief. Today, He still seeks and saves the lost, and many are certainly glad for that.

Gold Nugget #3

"If you call out for insight and cry aloud for understanding, and if you look for it as for silver and search for it as for hidden treasure, then you will understand the fear of the Lord and find the knowledge of God."
—Proverbs 2:3-5

The apostles were undoubtedly impacted by Jesus' sense of purpose. In Acts 6, they had determined what their purpose was, and they could not be diverted from this purpose to wait on tables. As time went on, each apostle saw more clearly that they were to devote themselves to prayer and the Word. This basic purpose never changed, even though they carried it out in different places and in different ways. But through it all, they turned the world upside down because they were men of purpose.

The apostles didn't just decide to "make things happen." They cooperated with the will of God that existed for their life before the world began. And the Holy Spirit led them and worked in them to bring about fantastic results. Not only did the apostles know their purpose, but they could also plainly state it. Look at Galatians 2:7-9:

> They saw that I had been entrusted with the task of preaching the gospel to the Gentiles, just as Peter had been to the Jews. For God, who was at work in the ministry of Peter as an apostle to the Jews, was also at work in my ministry as an apostle to the Gentiles.

Paul knew his purpose, and he also knew Peter's purpose. Each one's mission was so well defined that others knew what it was and respected it. In fact, Paul's purpose was so clear to him that he refused to baptize people. In 1 Corinthians 1:14 and 17, he states, "I am thankful that I did not baptize any of you...For Christ did not send me to baptize but to preach the gospel." (Now I don't feel so guilty about not wanting to do hospital visitation! Furthermore, in Romans 15:20 and 22 Paul wrote,

> It has always been my ambition to preach the gospel where Christ was not known, so that I would not be building on someone else's foundation . . . This is why I have often been hindered from coming to you.

Paul's mission was to preach to the Gentiles who had never heard of Christ. When he tried to go to Rome, a trip that at the time was not consistent with his purpose, God resisted him!

Paul loved that church, but for him Rome was the equivalent of "waiting on tables." The only way he thought he would get there was stated in Romans 15:24: "I plan to do so [visit the Roman church] when I go to Spain. I hope to visit you while passing through." Paul thought he could get to Rome as he went to the unevangelized people of Spain. Instead, he got there after he appealed to Caesar, since evangelizing kings and leaders was part of his purpose.

You have a purpose, just like Adam, Abraham, David, Daniel and Paul. Ephesians 4:16 says, "From whom the whole body, joined and knit together by what every joint supplies, *according to the effective working by which every part does its share*, causes growth of the body for the edifying of itself in love" (NKJV, emphasis added).

The word "effective" in that verse means that each part supplies what only it can supply. When that happens, the Body is effective. And remember, Adam, Esther, and Daniel didn't function as religious leaders and you may not either. But you will strengthen the Body by being who God made you to be, even though your main thrust may be in another sphere of life.

John Wooden, legendary college basketball coach at UCLA, once said, "Do not let what you cannot do interfere with what you can do." Don't feel as if you need to be everything to everyone. You don't have to do all the ministry. And you don't need to be president of the company to be successful. You just have to be faithful to your purpose and please God by so doing.

Think of this analogy from the sports world. No football team wants a quarterback who can do it all. The quarterback doesn't need to also be the defensive back, tight end, and halfback. What the team wants and needs is a quarterback who can throw the ball and lead the team downfield. It's the same with the body of Christ. The body of Christ doesn't need well-rounded people. The Body needs people who are specialists, who know their purpose and have given themselves to it wholeheartedly.

In secular circles, this emphasis is called building on strengths and minimizing weaknesses. Marcus Buckingham, unofficial leader of the strengths movement, defines a strength as something you do that leaves you feeling exhilarated or "strong." He also points out that a weakness leaves you weak after you perform it, no matter how skilled you are at doing it. That explains my dislike for hospital visitation. I could do it (and knew how to perform my duties well), but it left me drained when I did.

Let me also interject that there is a difference between your gifts and your purpose. Your gifts are the tools you have to help you fulfill your purpose. I plumber has a tool box and in it is a wrench. The plumber's purpose is not to wrench, that's the tool. The plumber's purpose is to fix your pipes. I have gifts of teaching, humor, administration, writing, and administration (I know I listed that already, but it's a big gift!). Those gifts help me fulfill my purpose, but they are not my purpose.

First Corinthians 3:13 says, "His work shall be shown for what it is, because the Day will bring it to light. It will be revealed with fire, and the fire will test the quality of each man's work." The fire will test your work. I have often wondered if burnout is a result of the fire of God that tests your work every now and then. This fire may reveal something you are involved in that you don't need to be involved in. That activity takes more energy than it gives. If you can identify what you still have energy to do while suffering from burnout, you're well on your way to knowing what your life purpose is. The work you did out of guilt, anxiety, pride, or ignorance burns up like wood, hay, and stubble.

When I hear that someone is battling burnout—and it is quite common, especially among those in ministry—I often refer to the burning bush in the story of Moses. I am sure Moses had seen other burning bushes in the wilderness, but the one that got his attention was the one that burned but was not consumed. That is how you should be in your purpose. You should burn brightly, but never be consumed, always having energy to flow in purpose.

By now, you are probably asking, "How exactly can I identify my purpose?" With that question in mind, let's look at some simple steps that you can take to clarify your life purpose.

Chapter 4

Finding the Road That Leads to Your Purpose

There's an old proverb that says, "The longest journey begins with the first step." In this chapter, we will outline the practical steps you can take to help you define your God-given purpose. They are the same steps that Nehemiah took to find and confirm what God called him to do. You may want to read the book of Nehemiah before you read this chapter. As you read, ask yourself, "How can I find this sense of destiny? How can I sort out my world and life as Nehemiah did, get to the place of purpose that he got to, and state my mission with certainty?"

After you have read Nehemiah, consider the following four points.

1. **Nehemiah sought the Lord for his purpose.** You may not be aware of your purpose because you've never asked the Lord to clarify it for you. Nehemiah 1:4 says, "When I heard these things, I sat down and wept. For some days I mourned and fasted and prayed before the God of heaven." It was in that posture that Nehemiah saw what God wanted him to do.

Perhaps Nehemiah was familiar with Proverbs 2:3-5, a Gold Nugget mentioned earlier: "If you *call out* for insight and *cry aloud* for understanding, and if you *look for it* as for silver and *search for it as for hidden treasure*, then you will understand the fear of the Lord and find the knowledge of God" (emphasis added). That's what seeking the Lord should look like.

Gold Nugget #4

"It is the glory of God to conceal a matter; to search out a matter is the glory of kings."
—Proverbs 25:2

You must cry aloud and earnestly seek the Lord with all your being. For instance, the congregation I once pastored set aside January for prayer and fasting. We usually fasted for 21 days and had regular prayer times. I was always amazed how God allowed Himself to be found during those times; He was faithful to reveal Himself in response to our diligent search.

The New Testament confirms what Proverbs 2 teaches. Hebrews 11:6 says, "Without faith it is impossible to please God, because anyone who comes to him must believe that he exists and that he rewards those who earnestly [diligently] seek him." If you seek the Lord with all you have, you will find Him. Or perhaps it's better to say that He will allow Himself to be found.

You may already know your purpose, or be closer to knowing it than you realize. Often it's the thing you see and say, "Wow, how did you do that?"? You probably reply, "It was nothing." In a sense, it was nothing to you because it was consistent with your purpose. For you it comes naturally, and for that reason you may consider it insignificant.

In fact, when I coach people seeking purpose, I am listening for two words: "just" and "only." When someone says "I *just* work with teenagers," or "I *only* enjoy working in the kitchen," I take notice. For when people minimize what they do, it is often because it comes so naturally that they tend to look right past it as they consider purpose. They are often looking for something more dynamic or more "unlike" them. They are expecting God to make them who they have never been. I advise purpose seekers with these words: "If you could not sing before, the probability of you singing now as you seek purpose is remote.

So let's focus on what you have done regularly even before you started seeking."

One other comment I often hear in coaching sessions is, "I have no idea what my purpose is!" to which I respond with amazement, "No idea?" and the person generally confirms, "No idea!" Then I begin to ask questions: "Do you want to be an astronaut?" to which the person responds, "No!" "How about a truck driver?" and again the person says, "No way!" "Then how about a surgeon?" and the response comes back, "Not a chance!"

It's then that I point out, "Well, if you had no idea, you would have to say maybe to those questions. The fact that you are so sure the answer is no gives me the impression that you know more than you realize!" After some additional questions, we have narrowed down the list to one or two things, to which the person will usually response, "That's it? I've been doing that all my life!"

Nehemiah's purpose, for example, was to rebuild Jerusalem, the city of his fathers, which is why he asked visitors how it was "back home." Everyone else was carrying on with business as usual, but Nehemiah had a burden for Jerusalem. The visitors' report that the city was in ruins devastated Nehemiah more than anyone else. That report simply helped make it clear to him what he was to do about that situation back home. My guess is that Nehemiah had been passionate about his people and his city for some time, but didn't recognize it for what it was. When he heard the report of the devastation, he was moved, started asking questions he had never asked before, and got answers he would not have been ready to receive prior to the report of Jerusalem's demise.

You don't have to make national headlines, preach like Billy Graham, minister like Mother Teresa, or sing like Amy Grant to be successful in the eyes of God. Consider Dorcas, whose death and resuscitation are described in Acts 9:36-43. Dorcas was a woman of means and a seamstress who "was always doing good and helping the poor." That was her purpose; she gave herself to it and did an effective job.

When Dorcas died, her friends summoned Peter, the apostle to the Jews and arguably the best known apostle of the day. He was a powerful man of God who went to pay his respects to a small-town seamstress. When he arrived at her house, he found everybody weeping. The widows showed him the clothes Dorcas had made for them, proof that she had faithfully carried out her mission. Peter was so moved by a woman given to her purpose that he went in, prayed, and told her to "get up." Dorcas, who ministered to an insignificant group of people in a nowhere town, received all the resources of heaven in her hour of need because she had been faithful to her God-given purpose.

I wonder if Dorcas ever thought, "The only thing I know how to do is sew. That cloak was nothing. Please accept it as my gift." Perhaps she thought that what she did was nothing special, but in reality, her handiwork was the result of divine empowerment. She did what she did best and blessed many people through her purpose. You have the same potential.

How about a man named Joseph who is mentioned in the Book of Acts? You probably don't know him as Joseph, because his name was changed by the apostles. This Joseph gave himself wholeheartedly to his purpose so that people took it upon themselves to change his name!

We read in Acts 4:36-37 "Joseph, a Levite from Cyprus, whom the apostles called Barnabas (which means Son of Encouragement), sold a field he owned and brought the money and put it at the apostles' feet."

Put yourself in the apostles' place in those early days. Maybe they had a rough day, and the secretary informed them they had one appointment remaining. When they heard it was Joseph, they said, "Oh, you mean Barnabas, the Son of Encouragement. Every time we see him he encourages us. Show him in."

At that point, Joseph came in holding two bags of money and placed them at the apostles' feet. He said, "I had this piece of land and I thought I would sell it and give the money to you to do with as you wish. I appreciate the job you're doing and I love you all." When he left, the apostles were glad they had let him in. He refreshed and encouraged them and was true to the new name he had been given. From that point on, every time we read of Barnabas, he is living up to his name, which embodied his purpose to encourage.

When the early church would not have anything to do with Saul, Barnabas came forward and encouraged them to accept him (Acts 9:27). When the work in Antioch among the Gentiles was exploding, the apostles sent Barnabas there:

> When he arrived and saw the evidence of the grace of God, he was glad and *encouraged* them all to remain true to the Lord with all their hearts. He was a good man, full of the Holy Spirit and faith, and a great number of people were brought to the Lord (Acts 11:23-24 emphasis added).

Barnabas wasn't interested in keeping that work in Antioch all to himself, so he "went to Tarsus to look for Saul, and when he found him, he brought him to Antioch" (Acts 11:25-26). Barnabas took that opportunity to encourage Saul and his ministry after he encouraged the new church at Antioch.

Barnabas had more than a gift of encouragement. Even though he was a teacher, apostle, prophet, evangelist, and giver, he encouraged people in the midst of it all. When he ran to encourage people, he felt God's pleasure.

Bolles in *What Color is Your Parachute?* writes,

> We need to unlearn the idea that our unique Mission must consist of some achievement which all the world will see, and learn instead that as the stone does not always know what ripples it has caused in the pond whose surface it impacts, so neither we nor those who watch our life will always know what we have achieved by our life and by our Mission. It may be that by the grace of God we helped bring about a profound change for the better in the lives of other souls around us, but it also may be that this takes place beyond our sight,

or after we have gone on. And we may never know what we have accomplished, until we see Him face-to-face after this life is past.[3]

I doubt if Dorcas expected to be memorialized in the written word of God for all generations because of what she did. But she was, and we are the richer for her story.

Nehemiah operated in the same power that comes when anyone functions in purpose. He sought the Lord for his purpose; in fact, he agonized over it. You can't read his opening prayer in Nehemiah 1:5-11 without feeling his agony as he poured out his heart before the Lord. He was diligent to seek and the Lord revealed his purpose.

2. **Nehemiah saw himself as part of a larger group**. Nehemiah didn't pray I prayers; he prayed we prayers. He said things like, "I confess the sins we have committed against you," "We have acted wickedly," and "We have not obeyed your commands." His fathers and grandfathers had abandoned the covenant, and as a result Nehemiah was serving in a foreign land, far away from Judah, through no apparent fault of his own. In spite of that reality, he was still praying "we" because he saw himself as part of a larger body.

Gold Nugget #5

"He who separates himself seeks his own desire, he quarrels against all sound wisdom."
—Proverbs 18:1

You need to see yourself in the same way. If you find yourself fulfilling your mission in the secular world, be a team player. Don't stand off and judge those with whom you work. Be a part of their lives and have the best interests of the organization at heart. Nehemiah served a heathen king and appears to have done it with distinction. Daniel gave his best to Nebuchadnezzar, the man who had ransacked his nation and radically changed his life. God expects you to give your best to your "world" as well, even if it is part of the world's system.

I learned this when I was secularly employed prior to entering the ministry. I found myself working at a chain of trade schools as the admissions director, and some of the students and coworkers had some serious problems. With those problems came the smoking, cursing, and perverted lifestyles that are all too common in the world.

I had a serious problem with one of my supervisors whose lifestyle was one that I found particularly troublesome and offensive. This man would order me to do things, yelling out my name from down the hall in a mocking tone. I tried to stay away from him as much as possible, but our paths still crossed more often than I liked.

While on this job, I was paid a commission, only to have my commissions dry up about one year after I took the job. I began praying for my financial needs and the Holy Spirit revealed to me that my bad attitude toward that supervisor had caused my financial lack.

I tried to reason with the Lord, but He would not relent. My finances did not improve until I repented of my attitude toward that man. When I did, not only did my finances improve, but my ability to work with my supervisor and other people improved. I saw how judgmental I had been, and I realized some of what Jesus must have encountered when He came to us. The sinless Son of God had to deal daily with imperfect men and women, yet He did so with grace and mercy. I was called to follow in His footsteps, and that job and supervisor gave me the perfect chance to do just that.

If you have found your purpose being fulfilled in church work, you too need to have the correct attitude. The Church is the apple of God's eye. Jesus didn't give Himself for you to stay in individualism. He gave Himself to build the Church. It's the Church that the gates of hell will try to prevail against unsuccessfully. There are many hurt people today who were wounded in church splits due to selfishness and poor leadership. Without question, there have been serious problems with leaders, elders, pastors, deacons, and staff members.

If you've been hurt, you need to follow Nehemiah's example and work through your hurt and anger to a place of healing and release. Then you need to get on with your purpose, which may take place for you in and through the Church. There's an entire generation today that doesn't really care what you've been through. When you compare what you've been through to the hell where they're going, you can see the importance of finding and functioning in your purpose. You also understand why the evil one has attacked the Church to render her weak and without purpose.

You may be thinking, "You don't know...I did so much... and the pastor brought his brother-in-law in and fired me. It was so unfair and painful." That's the way it can be when you are involved with imperfect people. It may not have been fair, but that's life in the real world. The Church has been an imperfect place filled with imperfect people for 2000 years, and it's not going to change any time soon. The Bible is full of instructions on how to handle your hurt. Withdrawal and isolation are not among your options.

I can relate to some of your pain and disillusionment in this area as well. Many years ago, I was "let go" from a Christian ministry. I had given a few years of my life to it, and then I was out. I reacted in anger, moved my office equipment home with no help, and found myself sitting in my office at home every morning pouting and depressed.

One morning the Holy Spirit spoke to me as clearly as He ever had and said, "You're not dealing with that ministry; you're dealing with Me. I sent you home." That statement saved my life and delivered me from destructive bitterness and anger. All of a sudden I saw that God had released me from that job because I wasn't needed there anymore. He had something else for me to do—a new way to apply my purpose—and He used that incident to get me in position for my next step. If I had been listening more closely to Him, I probably would have resigned before I was let go. I wasn't listening, however, and God had to use extraordinary means to get my attention.

Shortly after that release I got an invitation to pastor a church in Orlando, Florida, where I served for four wonderful years. I wrote this book in Orlando, where I was pastoring in a city I loved, surrounded by people I loved, and doing things I always dreamed of doing!

I was dealing with God—and you have been, too. God loves His Church and wants you to love it, too, regardless of what has happened. Whether you were hurt attending or working for a church, you need to have the same attitude as Joseph toward those who have hurt you. He told his brothers, "You intended to harm me, but God intended it for good to accomplish what is now being done, the saving of many lives" (Genesis 50:20).

Compare that with what Nehemiah could have said: "My fathers sinned and they did these things wrong." No! Instead he prayed, "We, we, we!" Because he had a right heart attitude, God clearly revealed to him that he was to have a role in the re-building process. Only "we" people get that privilege.

3. **Nehemiah confessed his inability to accomplish his purpose.** When I hear someone talking about purpose, I like to sense some humility. You must realize that God doesn't want you to trust in your own abilities, but in Him. If there is no awe for the purpose, there at least needs to be a healthy respect for the obstacles that must be overcome to accomplish it. God will not place you in your comfort zone. Your purpose will require faith and diligence if you are to be effective.

Nehemiah went to Jerusalem and surveyed how much needed to be done. His enemies rose up to discourage him, but he told them, "The God of heaven will give us success" (2:20). He had to pray constantly and ask God's help. The people had to work with a sword in one hand in case of attack. When they finished the wall in 52 days, Nehemiah wrote that "all the surrounding nations were afraid and lost their self-confidence, *because they realized that this work had been done with the help of our God*" (6:16, emphasis added). He knew that his effectiveness was found in God helping him do what he was created to do.

Abraham was certainly overwhelmed by his purpose to

be a father of a multitude. Moses came to the place where he could not lead the people without God's help. Solomon prayed for wisdom to lead Israel. Jeremiah tried to escape doing what he was to do, and God had to deal with him severely.

Everyone in the Bible was overwhelmed by their purpose. Even Jesus sweat drops of blood when He came to the hour in which His purpose would be fulfilled. Angels came and ministered to Him in the garden to strengthen Him for the cross, but still the burden was almost too much.

In light of this company, do you think that your purpose will be a trip down easy street? In all probability, it will take you out of yourself as you press into the Lord like never before—and cause you to realize your need for others more than ever before as you face your own limitations.

4. **Nehemiah was able to clearly describe his purpose to the king**. If you aren't clear about your purpose, other people won't be clear about it either. You need to have a statement that explains your purpose in one clear, concise sentence. Until you have that, you can't be fully effective because your focus will not be sharp and clear. You will still have the tendency to be distracted or spread too thin.

Nehemiah, the king's butler, came before the king with a sad face. The king asked, "Why does your face look so sad when you are not ill?" (2:2). Nehemiah responded that he was upset over the state of affairs in Jerusalem. The king then asked the crucial question, "What is it *you want*?" (2:4, emphasis added).

I'm glad Nehemiah didn't back down, or play religious games and say something like, "I just want the Lord to use me." Instead, he asked to be sent to the city of his fathers! He further requested supplies and letters of passage. The king finally asked, "How long will your journey take?" and Nehemiah "set a time" (2:6). He was specific. He knew what he was to do, what he needed to accomplish, and how much time it would take to finish it. He was specific in prayer and with men because he knew his purpose.

Clarifying my own purpose came as I went through a

painful failure a number of years ago. At that time, I was part of a team that started a "Christian" business. Our goals for our profits were simple and direct: We were going to make money for the kingdom of God, fund missions projects, and provide jobs only for the brothers and sisters in the church. With those goals, we just knew we couldn't fail, for God would certainly be with us.

We started the business and things went sour more quickly than we could ever have imagined. We spent $25,000 with very few sales to show for it. Soon all those involved went to look for other work. The business folded shortly thereafter, and because my name was on the office and phone system leases, guess who got stuck with the bills?

One morning I was praying, "Oh God, save this business for Your glory!" I felt the Holy Spirit respond gently as the thought shot through my mind, "You're not interested in My glory. You're interested in saving your own neck." That was absolutely true, and I angrily responded to the Lord, "If You didn't call me to start this business, then what did You call me to do?"

Immediately, I felt impressed to turn to Genesis 1:2, which says, "Now the earth was formless and empty, darkness was over the surface of the deep, and the Spirit of God was hovering over the waters." When I studied that verse in a commentary, it stated that the Spirit brought order out of the chaos found in the earth's condition. Suddenly, I was confronted with my own purpose: to create order out of chaos.

I almost fell to the ground. It was so clear, concise, and direct—and it made sense. When I was a child, I would empty my dad's garage, sweep it out, put everything back in order, and then feel an awesome sense of peace when I stood back and looked at everything in place. That tendency continued as an adult as I realized that every job I ever had was a job no one else had done. I was always given new positions so that I could create order out of chaos. Even before I was a believer, I was fulfilling my purpose and didn't know it! Creating order out of chaos was my life purpose!

Perhaps you are thinking "That doesn't seem very

specific. That doesn't really tell me what you do," and you would be correct. This purpose statement doesn't tell me what I should do, it indicates the effect I bring in whatever it is that I do. So when I consult, I create order out of chaos. When I write, I create order out of chaos. When I teach, I create order out of chaos. Purpose is not the job you do, it's the essence of who you are that comes through in all you do.

In John 7:38, Jesus said, "Whoever believes in me, as Scripture has said, rivers of living water will flow from within them." Part of this living water is your purpose as you express and live your life as no one else has or can. The water that emanates from you should not be bitter or salty, but it should taste like your brand and flavor. If you love color, then everything you do will be colorful. If you write, you will use your vocabulary and write from your unique perspective of life. If you play, it will be games that express who you are.

I have likened your purpose to a set of spiritual fingerprints. Think about fingerprints for a moment. You have a mark in very limited space that distinguishes you from every other human on the face of the earth. What's more, you probably have prints that no one has ever had in the history of mankind, for it doesn't seem like God recycles them! How does God do that in such a small piece of skin, yet He does it, and the same is true for purpose. You have a unique purpose that no one has, and no one else can do it like you do.

In most cases, your purpose is accompanied by a verse or passage of Scripture that gives a biblical summary for what you were born to do. When Jesus was in the synagogue in Nazareth where he was raised,

> ...the scroll of the prophet Isaiah was handed to him. Unrolling it, he found the place where it is written: "The Spirit of the Lord is on me, because he has anointed me to preach good news to the poor. He has sent me to proclaim freedom for the prisoners and recovery of sight for the blind, to release the oppressed, to proclaim the year of the Lord's favor" (Luke 4:17-19).

After he sat down, he said, "Today this scripture is fulfilled in your hearing" (verse 21). Jesus had a passage that summarized what His purpose was.

When an invitation first came for me to be involved in prison ministry, I felt released to do so because there was a lot of chaos in the inmates' lives; that ministry was consistent with my purpose. A ministry I assisted in South America was in need of structure and purpose when I first got involved. My call to Orlando was to come and pastor the church because it needed definition and purpose. All these ministry opportunities fit into my purpose of helping organize lives and institutions that have little or no structure. None of them came because I chose them. When I work to create order out of chaos, I'm effective and have power to achieve results. You might say that when I work with chaos, I feel God's pleasure.

I know you desire that same clarity, but getting it isn't always an easy process. Let's turn our attention now to some of the major obstacles you face as you seek your mission or purpose statement.

Chapter 5

Roadblocks on the Road to Purpose

Finding your purpose is not always easy. Finding my own purpose came out of a painful business failure. In fact, the process can be so difficult that many don't even bother to search for it. Others don't want to be responsible for what they find. Still others don't want to be restricted because they enjoy "free-lancing"— doing a little of this and a little of that. Let's look at some of the roadblocks you may encounter as you seek to find and clarify your purpose.

1. **Don't confuse "tent-making" with your purpose**. I asked a young lady one time what her purpose was and she responded without thought, "I'm a secretary." I seldom challenge anyone when they express their purpose, but I do try to give them a different perspective to help them see it more clearly and specifically. I told this young lady not to assume that her job is her purpose. As she was doing, you are undoubtedly performing a job that pays your bills, but that doesn't mean you should take your identity from it. William Carey, the great missionary pioneer, once said, "My business is to witness for Christ. I make shoes to pay my expenses."

If people had asked Paul what his purpose was, I doubt that he would have responded, "I'm a tent maker." He did make tents, but his purpose was to preach to the Gentiles. He used tent-making to accomplish his purpose. What's more, Paul wrote

32

13 letters in the New Testament, but he did not mention his trade in any of them. Luke informed us that Paul made tents in Acts, his historical account of the early church.

Nehemiah wasn't a butler; he was the rebuilder of Jerusalem. Once you see your purpose, it will help you endure a job that may even be a source of frustration for you, for it is simply funding your life but doesn't define your existence. Having a proper understanding of your purpose will also keep you from feeling as if you're not serving the Lord just because you're employed in a secular position.

My wife's sister is a writer. When she was working for a Christian magazine years ago, she took a standardized spiritual gifts assessment because she was trying to clarify her purpose. Her test results showed that she was strong in missions and hospitality (which was a confirmation of what she had always enjoyed doing), and that stimulated her thinking. She began to ask herself how she could fulfill her purpose as a missionary while employed in Alabama. The Lord soon showed her how to serve college students from foreign countries, and she began to specifically target students from mainland China.

She doesn't see herself primarily as a writer, although that's how she makes her living. She's a missionary and has found creative, Spirit-led ways to do what she was born to do. In fact, today she leads an initiative that addresses human trafficking and is making a difference in China, throughout Asia, and in many other parts of the world. She uses her writing gift to carry out her purpose to let the world know about oppressed and persecuted people.

Married women are particularly vulnerable to this identity crisis because they tend to draw their purpose from their day-to-day activities and routine. Housekeeping and raising children can fall under the category of "tent-making." That's what consumes most of a homemaker's time, but are those activities her divine purpose? A woman's children or husband can be called home to heaven at any time. If that happens, is her purpose finished?

Anna found herself in this very situation in Luke 2:36-38.

She was married for seven years when her husband died. But her purpose didn't die with him. Instead, she served in the Temple and "worshiped night and day, fasting and praying." Anna was 84 years old when Mary and Joseph came to the Temple. She ministered effectively and waited to see the hope of Israel. Women have purpose before they meet their spouses and after they have children.

My wife enjoys the world of business. When our children were young, however, she stayed home with them. She was then and still is a wonderful mother and homemaker, and I greatly admire her. She was also a great pastor's wife. Yet she has a purpose that is beyond our home, and today it is expressed through a line of jewelry that she designed and markets throughout the United States.

It became obvious that her purpose was not to counsel, teach, or serve in the church nursery on Sunday because when she had to prepare a lesson to teach, we all suffered as she struggled with it. But my wife's purpose does lie in the world of art and creativity. My job as her "helpmate" was to clear the way so she could fulfill her purpose as I am to fulfill mine.

Her purpose came home clearly at a time when our children were young. She had a business idea and began to venture into the woods, drag home grapevines, and fashion them into round and heart-shaped wreaths of all sizes. One thing led to another and, before we knew what happened, she had grossed almost $8,000 in annual sales while working out of her kitchen making wreaths. God anointed her as she functioned in her purpose then, and today she has a national platform to display and sell her art.

2. **Don't underestimate your ability to work**. The 40-hour work week is a modern phenomenon, a product of technology, union negotiations, and the modern pursuit of leisure. If you work in the energy and power of God as you carry out your purpose, however, you can do more than you ever thought possible! You can work 16-hour days and still be effective. On at least one occasion, Paul preached all night because his purpose

compelled him to move on the next day. During that sermon, a young man sank into a deep sleep and fell to the ground from the third story because Paul preached so long (see Acts 20). But Paul raised him up and kept right on functioning in his purpose of preaching to the Gentiles. Paul wrote that he endured "in hard work, sleepless nights and hunger" (2 Corinthians 6:5).

Years ago I was pastoring a church of 100 people. That kept me busy enough, but I also found myself serving as church administrator for a church of 1,200. In addition, I had family responsibilities, and was involved in several community service projects. In the midst of all that, I was asked to consider being the administrator for another ministry without relinquishing any of the responsibilities I already had.

There was no way I could do it all, or so I thought. I began to seek the Lord about my many duties and what I should eliminate. One morning I awoke with 1 Corinthians 15:10 on my mind. I didn't know what that verse said, and I hadn't been reading Corinthians lately. I went right to the Bible and found the answer to the questions I'd been asking God: "By the grace of God, I am what I am, and His grace to me was not without effect. No, I worked harder than all of them—yet not I, but the grace of God that was with me."

We will discuss that more when we look at the Gold Mine Principle of time management and organization, but I learned through that experience that I truly can do "all things through Christ who strengthens me" (Philippians 4:19). The Lord was clearly telling me that there wasn't going to be any less to do. In fact, He increased my duties without taking any away. He wanted to teach me how to handle an enlarged sphere!

If God wants you to go back to school, for instance, don't say, "I can't because classes are at night, and I'll be away from my family. It will cut into this or that." Go to school. You may be concerned that you won't have time to study, but you won't know that for sure until you get into it. At one point in my life, I was pastoring a church, traveling as event coordinator for Worship International, serving as executive director for the Julio Ruibal

Foundation (a missions group stationed in Colombia, South America), and functioning as president of the board of Rivers of Living Water Prison Ministries.

At the same time, I was also working on my doctorate in pastoral ministry from Liberty Theological Seminary in Houston, Texas. I was the assistant scoutmaster for my son's Boy Scout troop, and I was able to attend many of my daughter's school activities (and she was involved in quite a few).

It was difficult sometimes to juggle all those activities, but they all came out of my purpose; I felt God had directed me to each of them so I could create order out of chaos. In order to do them all well, however, I had to let other things go. There wasn't much time for television, for example, and I couldn't watch as many sporting events as I had previously.

It was difficult, but it can be done. If I did it, so can you, because the same grace is available to you. Take a look at 1 Corinthians 3:13: "His work will be shown for what it is." The word "work" is the Greek word *kopos*. It literally means "a beating of the breast with grief." It is also translated as "intense labor united with toil and trouble." That is what comes with purpose—hard work with some measure of trouble, which will keep you humble and dependent upon Him.

Years ago, an issue of *Christian History* magazine was devoted to "The Golden Age of Hymns" and featured articles about the great hymn writers of the past. One paragraph in that issue captured my attention. It told of William Cowper, who composed 68 hymns in his lifetime; John Newton, who wrote 280; Philip Doddridge, who produced almost 400; and Isaac Watts, who wrote 697. Charles Wesley, however, wrote 8,989 hymns![4]

Wesley didn't have a laptop, iPad, or smartphone. He wrote some of those hymns on horseback while going from one revival to the next. Charles Wesley was a man who knew his purpose. He was effective, worked long and hard, and has impacted many people for more than 200 years!

John Wesley, Charles' brother, is known as the founder

of the Methodist movement. Again, *Christian History* magazine gives us insight into the secret of John Wesley's effectiveness by providing this quote from his journal:

> This being my birthday, the first day of my seventy second year, I was considering, How is this, that I find just the same strength as I did thirty years ago? That my sight is considerably better now, and my nerves firmer than they were then? That I have none of the infirmities of old age, and have lost several I had in my youth? The grand cause is, the good pleasure of God, who doth whatsoever pleaseth him. The chief means are, 1, my constantly rising at four, for about fifty years: 2, my generally preaching at five in the morning, one of the most healthy exercises in the world: 3, my never travelling less, by sea or land, than four thousand five hundred miles a year.[5]

We are then told that "during his ministry, John Wesley road over 250,000 miles on horseback, a distance equal to ten circuits of the globe along the equator. He preached over 40,000 sermons."[6]

Don't underestimate your capacity to work. Allow the Holy Spirit to be released as you carry out your purpose. There are songs to be written, degrees to be earned, musical instruments to be played, and new languages to be mastered. If you can see these as part of your purpose and find a way to release the grace and power of God, you will be effective!

3. **Don't pursue or pray for the purpose that you want or hope to have**. That is a serious hindrance to finding your true purpose. Churches get torn apart at times because the associate wants to be pastor and the youth director wants more responsibility. I've seen men and women quit their jobs because they felt the jobs weren't spiritual enough. You can sincerely feel that you know your purpose and yet be sincerely wrong. Sincerity is not the judge of accuracy.

This actually happened to the Apostle Paul. Look at Acts 22:12-21:

A man named Ananias came to see me. He was a devout observer of the law and highly respected by all the Jews living there. He stood beside me and said, "Brother Saul, receive your sight!" And at that very moment I was able to see him. Then he said, "The God of our fathers has chosen you to know his will and to see the Righteous One and to hear words from his mouth. You will be his witness to all men of what you have seen and heard. And now what are you waiting for? Get up, be baptized and wash your sins away, calling on his name." When I returned to Jerusalem and was praying at the temple, I fell into a trance and saw the Lord speaking. "Quick!" he said to me. "Leave Jerusalem immediately, because they will not accept your testimony about me." "Lord," I replied, "these men know that I went from one synagogue to another to imprison and beat those who believe in you. And when the blood of your martyr Stephen was shed, I stood there giving my approval and guarding the clothes of those who were killing him." Then the Lord said to me, "Go; I will send you far away to the Gentiles."

What was Paul doing in Jerusalem? I believe he was pursuing the purpose he wanted or hoped to have. To paraphrase Paul, he was saying, "God's going to send me to my people, the Jews. I am a Jew's Jew. I'm already here in the Temple. They all know I persecuted the disciples. They'll know something happened on the road. You see, Lord, this is what I want to do for You. This is where You can best use me and it makes the most sense to me. And by the way, this is also where I feel most comfortable."

God responded to stay there, and it will cost you something to be involved in a purpose or pursuit not ordained by God. You will be busy but not effective. As stated earlier, Proverbs 28:19 says, "He who works his land will have abundant food, but the one who chases fantasies will have his fill of poverty." You have a plot of land to work and it's called purpose.

It belongs to you and you alone. If you work it, God will give you all that you need to get the job done. Any other field is a fantasy for you and will trap you in unfruitful busyness.

When I pray about things related to my purpose, I get results. The Lord has given me cars, phones, laptops, books, travel opportunities, spiritual insight, and much more because I needed them to work my "land." When I have chased "fantasies" (such as the wrong business opportunity or hospital visitation), I've only gotten frustrated.

When I entered the ministry, I was one of the youngest members of a 20-man full-time staff. I remember thinking that 19 men stood in front of me before I would ever get a chance to minister. In 11 years, I seldom got to preach; but truthfully, I would not have had much to say. That "field" wasn't mine. One day, I was reading the local newspaper and saw an announcement for a meeting of the Public Relations Council of Alabama (PRCA). The words jumped out at me, and I sensed the Holy Spirit say, "Go to that meeting. That's your field."

Believe me, I didn't want to go to that meeting, because I knew there would be a lot of unbelievers there. I knew I would probably be uncomfortable around them, and they would surely be uncomfortable around me. In my mind, I had a complete scenario of what would happen the moment I stepped inside the door; yet I knew God was telling me to go, so I went.

The first person who saw me and realized that I was a visitor walked over and introduced herself. When I told her my name and that I was with a local church, she immediately tried to hide her cigarette and put down her drink. I don't know who was more uncomfortable—she or I! That afternoon I told the Lord that this wasn't going to work! But the Lord would not relent. It was three or four months before He "persuaded" me to go back again.

I started going to this group's meeting on a regular basis and gave myself to working that "field." Eventually I became president of the local chapter and then a member of the state board of directors. Over the years, I had the opportunity to counsel and pray with many of the members, and when I entered our church's magazine in a state competition sponsored by this organization, it won first place!

When I left that church to take another pastorate out of state, I sent the local PRCA members invitations to my farewell service. Some of them came and heard me preach. Whenever I did anything for that organization, the power of God was evident. There was no power for me to minister in my church—that was not my field. PRCA was my field, and it bore a lot of fruit. With the Lord's help, I was able to function in my purpose of creating some order out of chaos in that situation.

As mentioned earlier, God is working today as He did in Daniel's time. He wants to send you to the Nebuchadnezzars of your day. Nebuchadnezzar was probably a hot-tempered, foul-mouthed idolater. It's amazing that God was the one who sent Daniel to work with that king. Daniel's purpose wasn't fulfilled in carrying out the requirements of the law in Jerusalem. Daniel was a righteous man, but his purpose was fulfilled in Babylon. He became the chief of the Babylonian wise men.

Can you imagine what Daniel's business meetings were like? Can you see him at the head of the table conducting the meeting? Perhaps the meeting went something like this: "All right, we will now have our report from the necromancers. And next let's hear from the astrologers. What's going on in your sphere? What's going on over here with the soothsayers, and what are the wise men of Babylon saying?" Daniel had to put up with wickedness, foolishness, sin, and evil men. But that's where God put him. He excelled in the midst of it all and was exalted. After they all gave their reports, then Daniel got to give his, and he told them of the one true God. Perhaps some heard and responded to the truth.

I developed the *Life Is a Gold Mine* seminar in 1985 and presented it in congregations around the country. It was well received and seemed anointed, but suddenly the invitations stopped coming. I didn't teach the seminar again for several years. When I started teaching it again, it was for prison inmates!

Perhaps the invitations had stopped coming because I was teaching in those early years out of ego and pride. I was a great teacher who was finally getting his chance—or so I thought.

The seminar was restored to me when I realized that the Lord gave it to me to help me accomplish my purpose. *Life Is a Gold Mine* was given to me to create order out of chaos, not to inflate my already healthy ego. When I got that straight, I was able to get back to the business of teaching others about purpose.

4. **Wrong attitudes**. It's so easy to get distracted in today's world. The lure of money, success, and materialism can keep you from devoting yourself to your purpose.

I have a friend who was pastoring, and he was a good pastor. He had position, influence, and what most would consider a successful ministry. Yet there was something gnawing at him that he couldn't avoid. He didn't feel pastoring was his purpose. He eventually gave up the pastoral ministry and devoted himself to music. He began writing songs in earnest and today he travels the world, ministering in song, and teaching others how to embrace a lifestyle of worship.

Before my friend could come into his purpose, he had to give up a comfortable living as a pastor. Another pastor once told me that he would not leave the pastorate because he would lose his pension. I'm not sure that was an adequate reason to remain. As I mentioned earlier, you're a hireling if you work for money, no matter what your job. You should work to help establish and strengthen God's kingdom wherever He sends you. Your provision is His responsibility. He is committed to provide for you in any and every situation.

Don't let money, pride, success, fear, the acclaim of men, or ministry success keep you from fulfilling your purpose. A correct attitude is essential if you are to find your mission. When you find it, take whatever steps are necessary to carry it out.

5. **Don't focus on your purpose at the expense of your relationship with the Lord**. In Acts 13, Saul was finally released to the Gentiles. Acts 13:2 says, "The Holy Spirit said, '*Set*

apart for me Barnabas and Saul'" (emphasis added). The Greek phrase "set apart for me" is in the middle voice, which can denote someone doing something for oneself. The middle voice in this verse denotes that the Holy Spirit was calling them to their purpose by calling them to Himself. Your revealed purpose should never take on greater importance than your relationship with the Lord. If it does, God will resist you until your priorities are correct.

Paul understood this and wrote about it to the Philippian church.

> For to me, to live is Christ and to die is gain. If I am to go on living in the body, this will mean fruitful [effective] labor for me. Yet what shall I choose? I do not know! I am torn between the two: I desire to depart and be with Christ, which is better by far; but it is more necessary for you that I remain in the body (Philippians 1:21-24).

As important as Paul's mission was, he was ready to leave it to be with the Lord, for that was "better." He was content to stay on because it was useful to so many, but he was ready to leave it at any time. That attitude enabled Paul to be even more effective, since his focus was on the Lord and not on ministry or the people.

God doesn't need you. He does, however, choose to use you. Don't take yourself too seriously! After all, God spoke to Balaam through a donkey, and He can get praise from rocks if He so desires. Take God seriously and you'll develop an effective lifestyle. Take yourself too seriously and you'll become busy but not effective.

If you keep an eye out for these roadblocks, your journey on the road to clearly defining your purpose will be a smooth one. In the next chapter, let's look at some more simple steps that will help you write out your purpose statement.

Chapter 6

Steps to Help Define Your Purpose

We've already looked at Proverbs 25:2, which states, "It is the glory of God to conceal a matter; to search out a matter is the glory of kings." You're a child of God the King, and that makes you royalty. Part of your royal inheritance is to search out the things that God has chosen to conceal.

Richard Bolles wrote,

> The puzzle of figuring out what your Mission in life is, will likely take some time. It is not a problem to be solved in a day and a night. It is a learning process which has steps to it, much like the process by which we learned to eat. As a baby we did not tackle adult food right off.[7]

Since discovering your purpose is a process, it is helpful to consider the following questions and steps to help clarify your purpose. As it becomes clear, then commit yourself wholeheartedly to pursue it. That's the only way you'll be truly effective.

1. What did you do as a child, that you don't do any longer, that gave you the greatest joy? A woman in Kenya answered this question with the activity of knitting. She started knitting again at the age of 33, began making gifts for friends that other people wanted to buy, and today she has quit the job she hated to go into a gift business that now has four employees.

2. List any things you have done that were easy or

seemingly insignificant and for which people have complimented you. Your purpose can be so natural that you assume everyone sees life like you do or can do what you do so well. That is usually not the case, for your purpose will cause certain things to come naturally to you, but not to most people.

3. Identify verses of Scripture and Bible characters that have meant the most to you. Write them all down and see if there is a pattern. For example, David has always been special to me, because of the price he paid to lead his own people out of chaos into order.

4. Reflect on the earliest words or impressions you had from the Lord, for often they contain clues to your purpose. My earliest impression was a call to "full-time service." I realize today that "full-time" was a clue to the busy nature of my work and not to pastoral ministry.

5. Read my other books on the subject of purpose: *I Wrote This Book on Purpose, So You Can Know Yours*; *Unlocking the Power of Purpose*; *A String of Pearls: Wisdom for Productive People*; or *The Price of Leadership: Paying the Price to Be a Great Leader*. You can also check out my site www.stankomondaymemo.com, which has hundreds of weekly updates on purpose that I have been writing since 2001.

6. Check out my website www.purposequest.com, which has a lot of free material to help you identify and understand your purpose.

7. What is it you do that, when you do it, you "feel His pleasure"? What gives you your greatest excitement in life or work? If you have ever suffered from burnout, what did you still have energy to do?

8. Take all this material and work on a purpose statement with a one-sentence summary of your purpose. You will become more and more effective as you endeavor to do what is necessary to fulfill this purpose with excellence.

To help you further visualize a mission statement, I've included a draft of my own. You may structure yours differently, but I share it with the hope that it will stimulate you to write one from your own understanding and experience.

MY PERSONAL MISSION STATEMENT

I surrendered my life to Jesus Christ on May 18, 1973. The next day I received His call to "give my life to full-time service." From that, I have come to realize that my purpose in life is to create order out of chaos wherever the Lord chooses to plant me using Genesis 1:2 as my guide: "Now the earth was formless and empty, darkness was over the surface of the deep, and the Spirit of God was hovering over the waters." As the Spirit was present to create order out of chaos, so I will draw on the Spirit's wisdom, power, and gifts to do the same. To achieve this, I commit myself to:

1. Be a giver and not a taker (see Mark 10:45).
2. Produce more than I use (see Hebrews 5:11-14).
3. Sever the best interests of others and not my own (see Philippians 2:19-24).
4. Be an example of hard work and diligence (see 1 Corinthians 15:10).
5. Use my humor as the gift of God that it is (see Nehemiah 8:10).
6. Lead with compassion and follow with humility (see 1 Peter 5:2-4).
7. Continue to study and learn until I die (see Psalms 119:18).
8. Walk in faith financially (see Hebrews 10:35-39).
9. Be a source of godly wisdom (read the book of Proverbs).
10. Invest all I can in the lives of others (see 1 Thessalonians 5:14).
11. Be an example of order and discipline (see 1 Corinthians 14:33 and 2 Timothy 1:7).

12. Use the word of God as my guidebook for life and death (see 2 Timothy 3:16).

13. Help each member of my family find his or her purpose (see Proverbs 22:6).

This last list of 13 statements represent my governing values that I have written out and defined (more on those governing values in Chapter 21). They go hand-in-hand with my purpose, and tell me how to fulfill my purpose. You can find a document on my website to help you write out your own set of values. As we close this first section, don't be in a hurry to move on. Instead, linger in this section a bit longer to see how far you get in finding your plot of ground that we have called your life purpose. When you are done, it will be time to move on to the next Gold Mine Principle, which is the concept of creativity.

GOLD MINE PRINCIPLE #2

CREATIVITY

Digging in New Places

"I was there when he set the heavens in place, when he marked out the horizon on the face of the deep, when he established the clouds above and fixed securely the fountains of the deep, when he gave the sea its boundary so the waters would not overstep his command, and when he marked out the foundations of the earth." — Proverbs 8:27-29

Chapter 7

You Are Creative . . . And So Am I!

People often ask, "Can your purpose change?" or "Can you have more than one purpose?" I always answer no to both questions. A few years ago, however, my purpose statement changed. My purpose didn't change, but my statement did. First, I state that you cannot have more than one purpose; then I say my purpose changed. Am I confused? Have I changed my mind? The answer to both questions is no, but let explain and you decide for yourself.

For many years, I stated that my purpose was "to bring [or make] order out of chaos." Then one day, while working in Zimbabwe, I had an epiphany of sorts. I realized that this definition wasn't correct. It wasn't so much that the definition was incorrect, but the way I interpreted my purpose was. On that fateful day in 2003, I realized that I don't *bring* or make order out of chaos, rather I *create* order out of chaos. It dawned on me that I am a creative person and thus my statement should be [as has been since], "I *create* order out of chaos."

In the first two editions, I used the words bring and make, but if you go back and look in Section One, you will see that the word *create* appears with every mention of my purpose statement. What a difference one word has made in my life's work!

Up to that time in Zimbabwe, I had always viewed myself as an organized, administrative-type person. I saw musicians, songwriters, and poets as the creative people, while I existed to organize their creativity. On that day, I saw that my ability to bring order *is* in and of itself is a creative act. When I saw that I gave myself permission to be creative. That decision changed how I defined my purpose—and changed my life. This is so important that I have now edited the Gold Mine Principles to make room for their newest member, namely *creativity*.

Take out a piece of paper now and write down all the ways you are creative. Don't overlook activities like cooking, baking, gardening, floral design, letter writing, teaching, cleaning, repair work, interior design, and makeup and hair styling. To further help you with this, consider the following facts:

- I don't want to be offensive, but you were made to create other human beings. When you reach maturity and marry, in most cases you must take precautions to *limit* your creativity, your offspring.

- Scientists tell us that every seven years you have a totally new set of cells in your body. Your cells are constantly dividing and creating new cells.

- One of the first things I did when I returned home recently was to get a haircut. In most cases, your body is creating new hair, nails and whiskers (men only, I hope) on a daily basis.

- Your body is constantly creating what it needs to carry on life. Your stomach creates gastric juices, sweat glands produce sweat and your ears create wax!

- What happens when you go to sleep? You create dreams; you are a "dream machine." For every eight hours you sleep, you dream almost two hours. Your mind is constantly creating symbolic sleep scenarios that help you maintain your psychological equilibrium.

- Every day you create thoughts and ideas; you also

daydream, creating potential scenarios with your role in them.

- You talk every day, stringing words and ideas together creatively. Someone said there is a good chance you will utter a sentence today that has never been uttered in the history of the world.

In Section One, we looked at your fingerprints as a metaphor for your life's purpose. Those same fingerprints are also an expression of your unique creative ability. As you touch things creatively, you leave a mark that separates you from everyone else in history—just like it is for your life purpose.

Gold Nugget #6

"By wisdom the LORD laid the earth's foundations, by understanding he set the heavens in place; by his knowledge the watery depths were divided, and the clouds let drop the dew."
—Proverbs 3:19-20

Without even trying, you are naturally a creative being, but you may be hindering your own tendency to create, and your problem is the one I had: how I thought about myself. You have been conditioned to believe that you *aren't* creative, so it is possible to go through life thinking that you aren't and consequently not recognizing when you are being creative.

A few weeks before I saw this change, I was heading to Uganda with a team from my home city. On the plane, the team leader asked me to fill out a form outlining my goals and objectives for the trip. Then she asked me to do something that would normally strike fear to my heart: She asked me to draw three pictures on the back of the paper to depict myself before, during, and after the trip.

I actually felt my body stiffen as she asked me to draw those pictures, because "I can't draw," or so I thought. Right there on the plane I decided to face my fear of being ridiculed or of not being very good, and proceeded to draw three pretty simple but effective pictures. They were the first three pictures I had ever drawn as an adult that I could remember.

Then I took out a sheet of paper and listed all the areas in which I could be considered creative. Here is how my list read: humor, consulting, conference and event coordination, *The Monday Memo* (I have written almost 800 weekly Memos in 16 years), my weekly Bible studies (in nine years, I wrote a devotional for all 8,000 verses in the New Testament), my books (28 as of this writing), public speaking, my daily to-do list, my website and blog, the seminars that I teach, the public speaking I do, and the two businesses that I have started. These are all creative acts, so therefore I am creative! I *create* order out of chaos.

Gold Nugget #7

"The wise woman builds her house, but with her own hands the foolish one tears hers down."
—Proverbs 14:1

I am describing my journey to creativity awareness to show that you are creative, too. The Creator made you in His image and part of that image is to create. You may not see yourself as creative, but you are. You may not have any original ideas that have never existed in the history of mankind (who does?), but you probably have ideas of how to creatively apply concepts that already exist in new ways.

When you think you aren't creative, you won't produce or won't recognize your creativity for what it is. For many years, I saw myself as "only" an administrator who got things done. Now I see myself as an administrator who creatively gets things done. That slight change of thinking and speaking changed my life—and released my creativity.

I also say this to help you overcome any bias that you may have against your creativity. Stop comparing yourself to others and don't compare what you create with what others create. Let your creativity flow, just like I did with my three pictures I drew. Your creativity may hold a key to help you clarify your purpose.

A creative God created you to be creative, as explained above. Creativity is programmed into the very fabric of your being, and you express your creativity every day in many ways. To further prove this, let's go all the way back to the beginning, and that would be in the earliest accounts of man's creation in the book of Genesis. In the process, we will develop what I call a theology of creativity.

Chapter 8

Adam's Zoo

There is always much speculation about man's beginnings and how creation came about. God saw fit only to give us 10 chapters worth of explanation of what happened, and that's why we call it the book Genesis, which means "starting point." While those ten chapters don't contain all that we would like to know, it contains much that we need to know. The Genesis account provides the best explanation for who man is, why God created him, what His intention was for creation, what went wrong, and God's solution for the problem.

There are five characteristics of man's existence, as I see them, that were established and demonstrated in Genesis. Let's consider them in the order of their appearance.

Fellowship with God. Adam had a relationship with the Lord and they spoke openly and regularly: "God blessed them and said to them . . ." (Genesis 1:28a). This was not to be the exception, but the rule and God continued to speak and reveal His will throughout the Creation account.

Purpose. The first thing God said to Adam was regarding his purpose. Some call it the dominion mandate, but I see it as a purpose statement: "God blessed them and said to them, "Be fruitful and increase in number; fill the earth and subdue it. Rule over the fish in the sea and the birds in the sky and over every living creature that moves on the ground" (Genesis 1:28). Adam had a purpose assignment and it was not to be a perpetual gardener or farmer. It was to oversee the expansion and care for God's magnificent creation.

Creativity. Adam was made by God to be creative and we are Adam's children. After God created Adam, He invited Adam to enter into the creative process by naming the animals: "Now the Lord God had formed out of the ground all the beasts of the field and all the birds of the air. He brought them to the man to see what he would name them; and whatever the man called each living creature, that was its name. So the man gave names to all the livestock, the birds of the air and all the beasts of the field" (Genesis 2:19-20). Adam decided what the animals were to be called; it was an expression of his creative dominion in the Garden. More on this a bit later.

Teamwork. Once Adam saw that none of the animals were a suitable assistant and helper, God put him into a deep sleep and created Eve: "So the LORD God caused the man to fall into a deep sleep; and while he was sleeping, he took one of the man's ribs and then closed up the place with flesh. Then the LORD God made a woman from the rib he had taken out of the man, and he brought her to the man" (Genesis 2:21-22). This act created the first work/purpose team, and it was to be repeated again and again as God put together teams to fulfill His purposes.

Rest. God would direct Adam and Eve's work through His ongoing fellowship with them, and then they were to rest from their labors and reflect in order to maintain the proper perspective of who they were and who God is. Later, Jesus told us that this rest day, called the Sabbath, was not for God's sake but for man's. The Jews got this concept all messed up, and believers do the same to this day.

There you have the five concepts that were instituted in the very beginning of man's creation. We all know what happened right after that, however, and it occurred in Genesis 3 when Adam and Eve decided to break their agreement with God (some call it a covenant) and make a new deal with their newest best friend, the serpent. When they made that deal and ate of the knowledge of the tree of good and evil, we have what theologians refer to as the Fall.

The Fall was cataclysmic in its effects, and it marred

every one of the five concepts we just described. While it marred the fellowship with God, purpose, creativity, teamwork, and rest, the Fall did not do away with them. It just took them off course and perverted them at their core. The Fall could be likened to a computer virus that eventually worked its way through man's operating system and corrupted all the files. The computer still worked, but not as God had intended. The Fall is still mankind's biggest problem today, for it continues to wreak havoc with God's intended order and plan.

Notice that the five concepts did not disappear after the Fall. God was still speaking to Adam and Eve, so there was still fellowship. Adam and Eve still had purpose, but they would have to work much harder to get the results they desired, and that would affect their ability to rest. Their relationship with one another was also affected, and someone pointed out that Adam and Eve were not only hiding from God after the Fall, they were hiding from one another! And Adam and Eve were still creative, but as the book of Genesis progresses, we see that mankind's creativity is increasingly applied in rebellious ways. That creative rebellion is a full-blown revolution today.

Gold Nugget #8

"Let your eyes look straight ahead, fix your gaze directly before you. Make level paths for your feet and take only ways that are firm. Do not swerve to the right or the left." —Proverbs 4:25-27

God was not stymied by this setback, and while He explained to Adam and Eve the implications of what they had done, He made a promise that He would act to reverse the curse that had been instituted by the Fall when He told the serpent: "Because you have done this, cursed are you above all livestock and all wild animals! You will crawl on your belly and you will eat dust all the days of your life. And I will put enmity between you and the woman, and between your offspring and hers; he will crush your head, and you will strike his heel" (Genesis 3:15-16).

This statement is actually the first time the gospel or good news of Christ was preached, for God promised He would send some-one to reestablish the order He intended in Genesis 1 and 2.

We know today that this "someone" was Jesus, the second Adam, who gave His life to do what the first Adam did not do: Obey God completely. Paul told us in Colossians 1:16-20,

> For in him all things were created: things in heaven and on earth, visible and invisible, whether thrones or powers or rulers or authorities; all things have been created through him and for him. He is before all things, and in him all things hold together. And he is the head of the body, the church; he is the beginning and the firstborn from among the dead, so that in everything he might have the supremacy. For God was pleased to have all his fullness dwell in him, and through him to reconcile to himself all things, whether things on earth or things in heaven, by making peace through his blood, shed on the cross.

Christ came to reconcile all things to the Father through His shed blood on the cross. Paul did not say most things, or some things, but all things. What would be included in those "all things"? I maintain that the five concepts described above would and should be numbered among the "all things." The problem is that the Church has restricted their work of reconciling to one of those "all things," and that is fellowship with God. If you come to Jesus, your sins will be forgiven and you have access to God. That is certainly true and important, but what about purpose? What about creativity? What about teamwork and rest? How many messages have you ever heard preached about those issues?

The point is that God is concerned not only about your relationship with Him, but what you will do after you are prop-erly related. He wants you to have purpose, be involved with others in work and ministry teams, and learn to rest as you trust His provision as you fulfill your purpose. He also wants you to reconnect with your creativity and, under His supervision, to allow it to express itself in ways that will glorify God and fulfill your deep need to be purposefully creative.

Too often, we have identified only musicians, songwriters, poets and writers as creative—and they are indeed creative. Those expressions, however, are only a few of the creative expressions that are available to Adam's children. As we did in the previous chapter, here are some additional creative expressions that are available to you:

Child raising—Raising a child requires tremendous creativity as you teach, train, entertain, and discipline each child according to his or her personality and needs.

Handwriting—Do you have beautiful handwriting? Then stop using the computer. Use your creative, artistic flair to communicate with others in your own writing.

Dress—You may have an eye for color or fashion. Be creative and adorn your body, God's creation, in a manner that is distinctive and uniquely you.

Repairs—It takes creativity not just to invent or design something, but to keep it in working order. Your ability to read a manual and then fix something is an expression of your creativity.

Gardening—Do you like flowers? Enjoy raising vegetables? Then plant to the glory of God and do it with your style and grace. If you don't plant the seeds, they won't grow! So join in the creative process and do what Adam and Eve did in the Garden. (Don't forget to pull the weeds, too!)

Time management—Can you organize your time and activities? That requires creativity. Can you help others organize? That requires even more creativity. We will look more closely at time management in Section Four.

Problem-solving—Do you face new problems and apply timeless wisdom and solutions? Then you are not just organized or efficient. You are creative!

I hope you get the picture. Like Adam, you are creative and God wants and in some ways is relying on you to express your creativity in everyday life. Stop saying you aren't creative—you are! I have assembled a list of creative expressions from past studies on creativity and that list is posted on my website. Take a look at that list and see how many expressions are present in your life, and then settle once and for all your attitude toward your own creativity.

Chapter 9

Old Testament Creativity

As we continue to develop a theology of creativity, we see in Genesis after the Fall that man's creative expressions continued, even if they became increasingly self-centered and less God-directed. The exception of course was Noah who built a magnificent boat from God's plans. After the Flood in in Genesis 10, we read about a man named Cush, who was a mighty entrepreneur and kingdom-builder:

> Cush was the father of Nimrod, who became a mighty warrior on the earth. He was a mighty hunter before the Lord; that is why it is said, "Like Nimrod, a mighty hunter before the Lord." The first centers of his kingdom were Babylon, Uruk, Akkad and Kalneh, in Shinar. From that land he went to Assyria, where he built Nineveh, Rehoboth Ir, Calah and Resen, which is between Nineveh and Calah—which is the great city (Genesis 10:8-12).

In Genesis 11, man's rebellion came full circle as he refused to "spread out" as God commanded, choosing rather to build a tower to heaven to make a name for himself. God thwarted those efforts by confusing their language so that they could not understand one another. Shortly thereafter, the Bible begins to tell the story of how God fulfilled His promise to the serpent that He would place enmity between him and Eve's offspring, and the story starts with a man named Abram, who was to become the focus for God's redemptive promise.

A Creative Strategy

There are many creative expressions that we could look at here, but I want to look at an unusual story involving Abraham's grandson by the name of Jacob. Jacob was a shrewd businessman who found himself working as a shepherd for his equally shrewd Uncle Laban. As Jacob prepared to leave his uncle, he negotiated a deal that would allow him Jacob to have all the speckled and spotted sheep in the flocks.

To Laban's surprise, Jacob proposed that all the existing spotted and speckled sheep be taken from the flock and only the yet-to-be-born spotted and speckled be Jacob's. What a strange plan, for how could Jacob expect to gain any sheep-with-designs if they were all removed before they could mate and reproduce? Laban was all too happy to comply and put a three-day's journey between his flocks and Jacob's so there would be no possibility, or so he thought, of Jacob getting any of his sheep.

But Jacob had a divine plan, a flash of brilliance and creative insight, that made him a wealthy man. We read in Genesis 30:37-43:

> Then Jacob took fresh rods of poplar and almond and plane trees, and peeled white stripes in them, exposing the white which *was* in the rods. He set the rods which he had peeled in front of the flocks in the gutters, *even* in the watering troughs, where the flocks came to drink; and they mated when they came to drink. So the flocks mated by the rods, and the flocks brought forth striped, speckled, and spotted. Jacob separated the lambs, and made the flocks face toward the striped and all the black in the flock of Laban; and he put his own herds apart, and did not put them with Laban's flock. Moreover, whenever the stronger of the flock were mating, Jacob would place the rods in the sight of the flock in the

gutters, so that they might mate by the rods; but when the flock was feeble, he did not put them in; so the feebler were Laban's and the stronger Jacob's. So the man became exceedingly prosperous, and had large flocks and female and male servants and camels and donkeys.

This strategy seems a bit unusual, but it worked. Later when Jacob was talking to his wives who were Laban's daughters, he said this in Genesis 31:10-13:

And it came about at the time when the flock were mating that I lifted up my eyes and saw in a dream, and behold, the male goats which were mating were striped, speckled, and mottled. Then the angel of God said to me in the dream, 'Jacob,' and I said, 'Here I am.' He said, 'Lift up now your eyes and see that all the male goats which are mating are striped, speckled, and mottled; for I have seen all that Laban has been doing to you. I am the God of Bethel, where you anointed a pillar, where you made a vow to Me; now arise, leave this land, and return to the land of your birth.'"

I don't understand how that worked, but Jacob had to follow through on the idea, however, to get the blessing. As an aside, I have found that often we are praying for money, but instead of money, God gives us an idea, and we have to convert that idea into action, and only then does the money come. There are no shortcuts and there is no winning a lottery. Jacob got the creative inspiration, had to implement what he saw, and over time he became wealthy. Do you have any creative ideas that you need to convert into action and then into cash and perhaps even wealth?

Filled with the Spirit

Yet there's more to examine as we develop our theology of creativity. What comes to mind when someone says that a person is "full of the Spirit"? Do you think that person must be in ministry, preaching, or prophesying the high things of God? Or do you think that person would be especially holy and sensitive to the Spirit's promptings? In most cases, you would be correct. There is a man in the Old Testament, however, whom God Himself identified as being full of the Spirit. That man was neither a priest nor was he engaged in some kind of priestly ministry.

The man I am referring to was Bezalel and he is mentioned in Exodus 31:1-5:

> Then the Lord said to Moses, "See, I have chosen Bezalel son of Uri, the son of Hur, of the tribe of Judah, and I have filled him with the Spirit of God, with skill, ability and knowledge in all kinds of crafts—to make artistic designs for work in gold, silver and bronze, to cut and set stones, to work in wood, and to engage in all kinds of craftsmanship."

Bezalel was a man skilled with his hands to do all kinds of handiwork. Notice that God filled Bezalel with His Spirit to create artistic designs and to work with metal, stones, and wood. He was so "anointed" at what he did that God chose him to do the work in the tabernacle, work that would be seen in its fullness by God regularly but by the high priest only once a year. What an honor!

Bezalel proves that God can equip and anoint you with His Spirit to perform your ministry outside the walls of your church. If this principle holds true today, that means you can be a banker, military leader, teacher, or politician who is full of the Spirit. Imagine being an "anointed" headmistress of a school or government official full of the Spirit. It's possible! Let me give you another example.

More on Bezalel

Before we move on, there's a bit more to learn from Bezalel's example. It seems that not only was Bezalel gifted and full of the Spirit of God to create, but others were empowered to help him carry out his duties:

> "Moreover, I have appointed Oholiab son of Ahisamak, of the tribe of Dan, to help him. Also I have given ability to all the skilled workers to make everything I have commanded you: the tent of meeting, the ark of the covenant law with the atonement cover on it, and all the other furnishings of the tent—the table and its articles, the pure gold lampstand and all its accessories, the altar of incense, the altar of burnt offering and all its utensils, the basin with its stand—and also the woven garments, both the sacred garments for Aaron the priest and the garments for his sons when they serve as priests, and the anointing oil and fragrant incense for the Holy Place. They are to make them just as I commanded you" (Exodus 31:6-11).

We have already discussed Bezalel's skill, but let's look at him and his work again from a different angle. God gave Bezalel and his colleagues great creative ability. My question to you concerning their creativity is this: Was their creativity optional, or was it their job, even their duty, to create? A second question is: If Bezalel and company had *not* created, would they have been disobeying the Lord? (Obviously, they would have been disobedient not to work on the tabernacle, for God commanded it, but I am talking about being creative in general, practicing and honing their creative skill over time.)

I ask those questions because some people treat their creativity as a hobby, something they will do when their real work allows. They will "get to it" when the kids are grown, or when they are under less pressure, or when circumstances are right. People with this attitude believe that it is the Lord's responsibility to make time for them and to create the circumstances that will allow their creativity to flow and flourish. If they get to it, fine, but if not, it's no great loss.

The answers to these questions are important, for they will help put creativity in its proper perspective, for it is not something to be pursued as a side interest but to be taken seriously. The other interesting point about Bezalel and company is that their creativity would not be seen by many people, for the tabernacle was the workplace of the priests, and the Holy of Holies was only seen by the high priest once a year. God did not assign just any artisans to work on what He would see; He assigned the best. God has every right to have you produce creative expressions for no one else but Him—neither for sale nor for the literary or artistic pleasure of others.

How do you view your creativity? Is it front and center in your life, or is it a side show? Do you work to make it better, or have you left it in its raw, primitive form? Do you see it as a mandate from the Lord, or something that you take or leave it at your discretion? I have made the choice to embrace mine as God-given, and have given it a place of priority in my daily life.

Creative Wisdom

As we wrap up our Old Testament theology of creativity, let's look at a passage about wisdom from Proverbs 8:30-31: "Then I [wisdom] was constantly at his side. I was filled with delight day after day, rejoicing always in his presence, rejoicing in his whole world and delighting in mankind."

Wisdom was at God's side when He created the earth. Therefore, if you want to be creative (or more creative), you need more wisdom. As we established earlier, wisdom for creativity does not require having a thought or idea that has never existed in the history of mankind. It is the ability to address new challenges and problems with a combination of new and existing knowledge. Take bottled water, for example. The developers invented neither plastic nor water. They simply applied and combined those existing entities to meet a need for portable drinking water. The equation for this process was as follows: need + water + plastic bottle x wisdom = a billion-dollar industry.

The implications of applying wisdom to the expression of creativity are tremendous, for you have already applied this equation to your life on a regular basis. For example, you take time + tasks + experience = your daily schedule. Or how about words + understanding of grammar + meaning + your unique perspective + your vocabulary combinations = speech and communication. You are a creative person and you express it every day. In fact, someone said that today you will string together some words and utter a sentence that has probably never been spoken in the history of mankind exactly as you will say it.

Gold Nugget #9

"By wisdom a house is built,
and through understanding it is established;
through knowledge its rooms are filled with
rare and beautiful treasures."
—Proverbs 24:3-4

While creativity does not require totally new concepts, inventions or ideas (although it can), it will involve your unique perspective on life situations that you face every day. No one else on earth looks at life and its events as you do. When you address those things, you will do so in a way that no one else has ever done. If you think, however, that you are not creative, you will miss your chance to contribute something new to the ongoing expression of life as you see and interpret it here on earth. You will simply tell others or at least think to yourself, "I am not creative" when you are a creative machine.

Are you ready to face, embrace, and express your creativity? What you need is not creativity, but the wisdom to express your creativity and that you can have in abundance, but only if you have faith: "If any of you lacks wisdom, you should ask God, who gives generously to all without finding fault, and it will be given to you. But when you ask, you must believe and not doubt, because the one who doubts is like a wave of the sea, blown and tossed by the wind" (James 1:5-6). I urge you to stop running from or misunderstanding your creativity, but instead ask for wisdom as to how to express it as you walk through your life assignment.

"His Anointed"

There is one final point to make in this chapter. In the book of Isaiah, the Lord refers to Cyrus, a secular king in the following manner: "Thus says the Lord to Cyrus His *anointed,* . . . I have also called you by your name; I have given you a title of honor though you have not known Me" (Isaiah 45:1, 4 emphasis added).

Cyrus was a king but was identified as anointed. In other words, God was with him when he ruled and governed, and Cyrus did so creatively. That truth leads to the question: What are you anointed to creatively do or perform? Is it teach school? Help the poor? Learn? Preach? Plan conferences? Edit manuscripts? Write? Don't limit your anointing to Church work, but take a look at what you do that, when you do it, you know God helps you.

Bezalel was a skilled craftsman and God was with him. Is God with you when you make jewelry, paint, sing, compose, or arrange? If He is, then you're full of the Spirit when you do those things, no matter where and for whom you do them. It's safe to say that you are anointed, just like Bezalel! That should motivate you to increasingly draw on God's help as you carry out your anointed purpose for His world in the coming days

Let's summarize the major points we have learned so far as we developed our theology of creativity:

- You were created to be creative, since you are made in the image of the Creator.

- You cannot help but be creative; you have to work to limit your creativity.

- Your creativity is often the source of your provision and even prosperity.

- It is the will of God that you express your creativity both in and outside of church settings.

The most important ingredient in expressing creativity is wisdom—learning how to use new and existing concepts and ideas to solve never-before-encountered challenges. Now that we have looked at creativity expressions in the Old Testament, it's time to move on to see what the New Testament has to offer where creativity is concerned.

Chapter 10

New Testament Creativity

We have looked at some examples of how creativity was expressed in the Old Testament as we seek to develop a theology of creativity, and now it's time to look at the New Testament. Of course, when you move to the New Testament, Jesus is front and center, so let's look at Jesus' life to see what He can add to our study of creativity.

Creator God, Creative Man

Not only did Jesus come to restore your creativity, but He Himself was a creative man, serving as a model for you to follow. If we attribute Jesus' creativity to His divinity, we can't gain much help or understanding that will assist us in our own creative endeavors. If we see, however, that Jesus was a creative man, then there may be things in His life to help us be more creative.

Let's start from Jesus' early life. We know He was a carpenter, so He made things from wood with His hands. One second-century bishop reported that wooden yokes Jesus made in the first century were still being used 100 years later! That tells us that Jesus wasn't only creative, He was also committed to excellence—He did good work.

There's a good chance that Jesus, as the oldest son, ran a carpentry business that supported more than just Himself. His brothers could have been in business with Him, and that means He also expressed His creativity by running a business in which he would make payroll, manage inventory and accounts, and handle customer service. He also would have supported His widowed mother from the business as well.

But Jesus' creativity didn't stop there. At the age of 30, He changed careers, starting an itinerate ministry through which He continued to express breathtaking creativity. His creativity was expressed in building and equipping an effective team of men and women who traveled with Him. When Jesus performed miracles, He did so with flair and distinction. One time He spit on the ground, made mud, and smeared it on a blind man's eyes. Another time, Jesus put His fingers into a deaf man's ears and touched the end of the man's tongue with His spit. Jesus answered His critics with creative retorts that delighted the crowds. His insight into Scripture held people's attention for days on end, and He impressed the crowd with His fresh approach to God and the Word.

Perhaps Jesus' greatest creative expression, however, was in His teaching. When He taught, He used parables—stories from everyday life that imparted truth. Where did He get those stories? He made them up, composing and crafting them to be effective teaching tools. They came from His creativity, perhaps the same creativity that He learned and perfected as a carpenter. Jesus used parables with lessons drawn from agriculture, business, current events, family life, and gardening. He was such a creative teacher that the people would walk for days to listen to Him for days, not giving much thought to where their next meal was coming from. Mark reported, "The large crowd listened to him with delight" (Mark 12:37).

Why is this important? First, Jesus' creativity did not emanate from His divinity only. He was and is the Creator God and creative man. On earth, He expressed His creativity as a Jewish man who observed life and saw God in all of it. Second, if Jesus the man was creative, then He can help us be creative. And finally, you will fulfill your purpose as you carry on the creative tradition that was expressed by the Son of God and continued in the power of the Holy Spirit. We are not here to maintain; we are here to creatively advance the kingdom of God. One might argue that our creativity is how we will fulfill the mandate given to Adam to subdue the earth and rule over it.

The Early Church

In chapter one, we looked at Acts 6:1-7 from the perspective of purpose. In that passage, we saw the apostles stayed true to their purpose by selecting men to carry the burden of the work among the widows. The people elected these men to serve or minister to the widows in the church, and the Greek word for service there is *diakonia*, from which we derive our modern church office of *deacon*.

Many churches have taken this passage in Acts 6 and turned it into a model for church government and service. In some churches, the deacons are the ultimate governing position; in others they are people who serve by doing practical things in the church like building care, women's ministry, and the like. The goal here is not to debate which approach to or interpretation of deacons is correct; the goal is to show that any approach to deacons as a church institution misses the point of the original story altogether. The original deacons were not about church government or tradition; they were simply a creative solution to a new problem.

As best I can tell, there was no biblical concept upon which the apostles drew to elect and commission the deacons. Jesus had instructed them to care for the poor. Most widows were poor in the early church if they had no other family to care for them. As the church grew, the number of widows grew from those outside the ranks of the Hebrew residents in Jerusalem. The apostles were being called upon to address this problem that had never before been faced.

They addressed this problem creatively and used wisdom to come up with a solution. I don't believe they were instituting a church office in Acts 6, but rather an approach the church should take to life's problems and challenges, whether in or outside the church. They were setting a precedent, not establishing a tradition.

When I think of creativity, I again go back to the verses we looked at in Proverbs 8:22-31. Wisdom was there at God's side when He created the universe. As we discussed in the previous chapter, wisdom is closely related to creativity, which leads to my definition of creativity: *the wise application of knowledge to existing problems or opportunities in such a way that something new emerges.*

In Acts 6, the problem was caring for the widows. The knowledge or biblical precedent that existed was the example of Moses appointing helpers to care for the people in Exodus 18. Another precedent was that elections were common in Israel to elect synagogue leaders. So the apostles applied existing knowledge—Moses appointing helpers and synagogue elections—in a new and wise way manner to address a problem they were facing. The result of their efforts was creativity as they appointed a group of men who we call deacons today.

The church—and the people in it—should be the bastion and vanguard of creativity. We have the creative Spirit of God in our midst. We should not be looking to solve new problems with the solutions of the past. We are bound to our traditions when we don't see creativity as a function of the church and believers, or when fear causes us to retreat to the tried-and-true *procedures* rather than experiment with new *applications* of tried-and-true wisdom principles.

I urge you not to settle for what's been done, but pioneer what's been done into what has never been done. The world is waiting for your poetry and your business ideas. The world is not waiting for us to debate the role of deacons, but to find 21st-century solutions to modern challenges that are the equal of what the apostles did in Acts 6. When you do, you will be working with the wisdom of Proverbs 8 that was present when God created and structured the world. There is no greater creativity with which you and I can work.

The Modern Church

Fortunately, there are many spiritual pioneers who understood this definition of creativity *as the wise application of knowledge to existing problems or opportunities in such a way that something new emerges.* For example, Robert Raikes saw the need for spiritual education of London's street children in the late 1700s and founded the Sunday School movement. William Booth wanted to minister to England's poor, so he started what we know today as the Salvation Army. In my book, *The Price of Leadership,* I highlight 29 men and women who I refer to as purpose pioneers who creatively impacted their generation through the creative expression of their purpose, people like Florence Nightingale, George Washington Carver, A. B. Simpson, John Wesley, and Sojourner Truth, just to name a few.

Then I read a book, *The Best American Spiritual Writing 2006.* One of the essays in that book, entitled "*Into the Wonder,*" was about C.S. Lewis, the well-known Christian author and apologist, and one of the great creative minds of the last century. That article has merit for this discussion on creativity.

The essay began by describing a particularly trying time in Lewis' life when he was living with his brother and an elderly woman. The woman was bedridden and increasingly used Lewis as an extra maid to help meet her needs. Meanwhile Lewis' brother, who helped him with correspondence and filing, drank himself to insensibility and ended up in a hospital. The pressures of this situation, along with his work load at Oxford, drove Lewis to the point of collapse and he was eventually hospitalized for exhaustion.

It was shortly thereafter that Lewis had a friend over so he could share a portion of a new children's book that Lewis was writing. This book became *The Lion, The Witch and The Wardrobe,* the first of *The Chronicles of Narnia,* which to date has sold 85 million copies in 30 languages. What is so interesting to me about this creative scenario?

First, Lewis wrote perhaps his most famous work at a most inopportune time in his life. I often feel like I can't be more creative or productive until certain things change, until my life is free of worry, anxiety or mental clutter. Lewis didn't wait for the best time. In fact, in a time of suffering and professional busyness, he began to write fiction for children, a most unusual exercise for a man known more at that point for his theological rather than fantasy work.

Second, Lewis was not married at the time and had no children. I think it's remarkable that Lewis could write so effectively for children when he had none of his own. Finally, Lewis was a loner as a child. His childhood, while not sad or abusive, wasn't filled with the kind of childhood joys upon which he could draw to write his stories.

Lewis produced creative work in spite of his personal difficulties. You must learn to do the same. You can no longer *not* create because circumstances in your life aren't quite right. Neither can you dismiss your creative ideas because you don't see yourself as qualified or fit. Lewis was neither a happy child nor natural father, yet he wrote children's books that changed the world. What could you do if you stopped hiding behind excuses and limitations and just did it?

It seems that Lewis' hardships prepared him to create; his suffering somehow fueled his drive to write. If you can see that your suffering is preparation and not a hindrance, you will find new freedom to produce when it may not seem like a good time to produce. And please don't tell anyone that you don't have the time to create. You have all the time in the world—24 hours every day. It's not that you don't have time; you aren't using it creatively to create. We will discuss that more fully in our section on the Gold Mine Principle of time and organization.

A Personal Testimony

In 2009, I reached a goal I set in 2001. I worked at that goal almost every day for more than eight years. What was my goal? What took me almost every day for nine years to complete? I completed a verse-by-verse commentary on the entire New Testament! (In case you were wondering, there are more than 8,000 verses in the New Testament and I wrote something for every one of them.)

After I completed a study of faith in 2001 (which later became my book *The Faith Files: Volume One*), I had an idea. I had always said that "one day" I wanted to write commentaries on the Bible. I decided to start such a study, determining that I would look at four verses every day (I have no idea why I chose four verses as my focus) and write some devotional material for those verses. At the end of every week, I would send out those notes to those who were already getting *The Faith Files*. The list continued to grow and today about 4,000 people still receive my weekly studies.

By studying and writing on four verses every day for eight years, I completed studies for all 27 New Testament books! Commenting on four verses a day every day enabled me to accomplish a huge task a little at a time. I exercised faith every day I sat down to write and I "saw" something in every verse along with ways to help the reader apply those verses to their daily walk. Needless to say, I have learned a lot since I began writing those studies and I hope my readers have, too. Now I am in process of publishing those studies, calling them the *Live the Word* commentary series.

How did I know I was supposed to embark on this project? Was I certain that it was God's will? I can't say for sure, but I refer you to what Luke wrote in the opening of his gospel:

> Therefore, since I myself have carefully investigated everything from the beginning, *it seemed good also to me to write an orderly account for you,* most excellent Theophilus, so that you may know the certainty of the things you have been taught (Luke 1:3-4 emphasis added).

All I can say is that it seemed good to me to write and keep on writing. As people would say they found the studies helpful, I just kept on going. The goal helped me reach the end. My creativity with God's help took care of the rest. I had faith for time, and I am glad to say that as far as my Bible studies are concerned, "It is finished!"

So what about you? Do you have any "good ideas" like I had? What can you accomplish if you do just a little every day? I have found that most people won't be *anything* because they can't see how to do *everything*. They won't give a *little* because they can't give a *lot*. They won't devote a little time because they don't have huge chunks of time. I decided to do what I could do every day four verses and now I have completed my creative project. There's no telling what you can do if you apply the same principle.

Chapter 11

Your Response to Creativity

━━━━━━━━━━━   ━━━━━━━━━━━

I recently received two emails from two people who were considering enlisting my services as a writing coach. Both emails were filled with fear as the people shared their approach to writing with themselves as the subject matter (fear of pride), of paying for the services (fear that God will not provide), and of whether or not their material was good enough to publish (fear of failure and inadequacy). One email talked about how it took all week to follow up on our initial correspondence due to "cold feet."

By now you realize the creative process is fraught with fear from beginning to end, and my experience of working with creative people has done nothing to change that conclusion. I am no longer surprised when I find fear in my own life, but instead I go looking for it, sort of like conducting a search-and-destroy military mission. I know my fear enemy is somewhere in my thinking. My job is to find where my fear and shame are hidden and camouflaged so they will not be seen for what they really are.

Why are we so riddled with fear? There is a biblical answer and, you guessed it, it's found in Genesis 3:7-10:

> Then the eyes of both of them were opened, and they realized they were naked; so they sewed fig leaves together and made coverings for themselves. Then the man and his wife heard the sound of the

Lord God as he was walking in the garden in the cool of the day, and they hid from the Lord God among the trees of the garden. But the Lord God called to the man, "Where are you?" He answered, "I heard you in the garden, and I was afraid because I was naked; so I hid."

Adam and Eve were afraid and ashamed of being exposed, so they hid from God. It's ludicrous for them to think they could hide from God, but they tried, and you and I try to hide as well. Adam and Eve covered themselves with fig leaves—flimsy coverings that would wither and die in a day or two—and we use flimsy excuses to hide our fear and shame. Those excuses sound quite rational, but they are nothing but fig leaves in our minds to mask the terror we face when we consider doing something creative or new. I read something recently that said Adam and Eve were not only hiding from God, but from one another. That is why we are fearful and ashamed to share our creativity with other people.

You may be nodding your head in agreement as you read this chapter. Yet, you can be in agreement and still be steeped in and paralyzed by your own fears, even denying their existence. Or perhaps you have learned to manage your fears by sticking to the beaten path of life, careful not to veer off into the jungle of the unknown, where you have never been before. Until you take that path less trodden, you won't have to face or even be conscious of your fears. What's more, if you can wrap your fear in spiritual-sounding excuses, phrases like, "It's not the right season," or "The Lord hasn't released me," or "I am waiting on a confirmation," then you can comfortably learn to live with your fear, convinced that it is God's will that you be content with your daily routine, medicating your mind with thoughts of what you will do "one day."

Where your creativity is concerned, you must accept the truth that *this* is the day that the Lord has made. You are not guaranteed tomorrow, so I urge you to face your fears today and move forward. We are children of Adam and Eve, and we all must take steps to emerge from the bushes of fear and shame so we can show forth the fullness of the glory that is ours in Christ. If you don't take those steps, then you will live a life far below what God had in mind when He sent Jesus to die for you.

Gold Nugget #10

"She makes linen garments and sells them, and supplies the merchants with sashes." —Proverbs 31:24.

Three Enemies

I have read all of the books on creativity and writing written by author Julia Cameron. While I don't agree with her theology (she is not a theologian per se, but has some unique thoughts on God and spirituality), I do agree with her that writing and creativity are spiritual experiences. In her book, *The Right to Write*, Cameron quoted the following artists concerning their creativity:

> "The music of this opera (Madame Butterfly) was dictated to me by God. I was merely instrumental in getting it on paper and communicating it to the public." - Giacomo Puccini

> "Straightaway the ideas flow in upon me, directly from God." - Johannes Brahms

> "The position of the artist is humble. He is essentially a channel." - Piet Mondrian.

> "I myself do nothing. The Holy Spirit Himself accomplishes all through me." - William Blake[1]

So if creativity is a spiritual expression (as some mention in the above quotes) and you are a spiritual person, why don't you create more? May I suggest three enemies that do battle with your God-given ability to create, and that battle occurs almost every time you sit down to create anything.

Fear. I know what you may be thinking: "John, we covered this already. Not again!" Yet fear is so powerful as the public enemy number one of creativity that we must address it in many different ways over and over again. How many fears can you think of that could prevent you from being creative? I can think of fear of failure, poverty, ridicule, family, culture, authority, inadequacy, and success.

I was visiting a church one November, and met with a woman who was a painter, but who was paralyzed with fear that prevented her from painting anything. We talked, prayed, and addressed the issue of fear. The next day she came in beaming and said she had a plan that was going to release her to paint and create again. I expressed my extreme pleasure and asked what the plan was. With all seriousness, she said, "I am going to paint starting next April 15!"

I went from extreme pleasure to extreme confusion, and asked, "Why do you need to wait until next April?" Her answer was simple: "That's when I get my tax refund check, so I can have the money to set up a studio!" She was afraid she could not create without her studio. She asked me what I thought, and this is what I said, "I have a different assignment in mind for you. Your job is to paint something and give it to someone as a Christmas gift." She then exploded, the shrapnel of excuses spraying the room: "You don't understand! I need my space. I need my colors! I cannot possibly do anything that would be worthwhile in the next six weeks!"

As I tried to talk her down from the ledge, so to speak, I began to show her how fear, which we had just discussed the day before, had once again reared its ugly head. When she saw that, she accepted her assignment and did create something quite nice in time to bless someone at Christmas.

If you are going to express your creativity, you must face and overcome the oppression of fear, just like that artist did. Fear will paralyze your efforts and cause you to procrastinate, while you wait for a more opportune time. Remember what Paul wrote his disciple Timothy: "For God has not given us a spirit of fear, but of power and of love and of a sound mind" (2 Timothy 1:7 NKJV). If you are afraid, what are you prepared to do about it?

Comparison. When you look at what you do and compare it to what others have done, it can cause you to stop being creative. In your opinion, you aren't "as good" as the other person. Stop and think about that. What is *good* where creativity is concerned? Isn't creativity a process and can't your simple efforts today lead to stellar creativity tomorrow? Is it wise to compare your initial or even mature efforts to what someone else may have spent a lot of time developing?

At the same time, you must realize that there is always someone who is more gifted, skilled, talented, beautiful, eloquent, prolific, coordinated, or disciplined than you are. When you encounter those people, they are to be admired and learned from as you seek to hone your own gift and skill. When professional athletes confront the superstars, they don't retire to the bench in anguish. They continue to play the game to the best of their ability and seek to learn from the more skilled player. What's even better is that the gifted players who understand the importance of a team can raise the level of performance for all the players on his or her team.

Paul described an important principle he used when he looked at his work: "We do not dare to classify or compare ourselves with some who commend themselves. When they measure themselves by themselves and compare themselves with themselves, they are not wise" (2 Corinthians 10:12-13). Why not do something creative this week and discipline yourself not to compare it to what anyone else has done? Is it the best it can be right now? If it is, then I would say you have done a good job.

Perfectionism. There is a little old man who has lived in you most of your adult life. He is very old and cranky. He has shriveled skin and wears a visor on his head, similar to the one worn by bookkeepers when they used adding machines instead of calculators and computers. This little old man has bony fingers and a scratchy voice that he uses to talk to you all the time. He doesn't have a name, but he has a role in your life that he plays to perfection. What is that role? It's the role of the critic, the censor, and the discourager.

When you write something, this little old man starts in: "You can't write. This is no good. I wouldn't show this to anyone. You'll never get this published!" If you try to take steps to improve yourself, the little man then says, "Who do you think you are? You're too old (or too young) to try to do something like this?" If you have an idea for a business or ministry, he chimes in and says, "That will never work. Why don't you just stay where you are, even though you're unhappy?"

Then when you become a Christian, that little old man takes on a whole new tone. "How do you know the Lord wants you to do that? Who do you think you are, Moses or Peter? There is nothing special about what you are thinking. What's more, you don't have the time, money, or spirituality to do it well. Just sit there and shut up. You know the mistakes you've made trying to do things in the past! All right, you did that once but you won't be able to do it again!"

There is no way I can describe all that this little man says or does in your life, but I think you get the idea. It is the voice of perfectionism and unrealistic expectations about what creativity is, and when it is ready to share with others. If you are going to clarify your purpose and be creative, you are going to have to deal with this little old man. I have found that you cannot reason with him, for he is too persuasive and persistent for that. The critic and censor in you will urge you to dismiss an idea within five minutes of when you first receive it. The critic in you will cause you not to talk about yourself and to hide your art and ideas. He will prey on your fears and cause you to compare yourself to those who are supremely successful, causing you to cower in despair as you behold your comparative lack of talent. So how do you deal with this little old man?

Jesus said, "The kingdom of heaven has been forcefully advancing, and forceful men lay hold of it" (Matthew 11:12-13). There is no nice way to deal with this little old man. You cannot have pity on him or listen to anything he says. I recommend that you poke this little old man in the eye whenever he talks to you! That's right, you must deal ruthlessly with him on every occasion that he decides to offer his two cents. You must say to him, "Thank you but you don't know what you are talking about." If he doesn't shut up, then you must occupy him by poking him in the eye. Just picture him holding his eye and bending over in pain. (Don't worry. He'll recover to speak again.) Then proceed to carry out the idea that you have while he is preoccupied, free from his annoying voice and tired accusations.

When you were young, that little old man didn't exist. You were free then to create, to be yourself, to have fun, and experiment with life. You did things just for the sake of doing them, and you learned and had fun. But as you got older, the old man took up residence to keep you fearful, bound-up, and failure-free. That little old man has taken something from you, however, and you must take it back, with violence if necessary. He took your youthful zeal for life, and with it he took your ability to create with freedom.

The pursuit of perfection is unrealistic and will hinder you from doing something great just because it isn't perfect. I can't find a verse that talks about perfectionism, but I can find one that speaks to excellence: "Whatever you do, work at it with all your heart, as working for the Lord, not for men" (Colossians 3:23). Perhaps the distinction between perfection and excellence will help you do something you haven't done because you feared it wasn't the best that was humanly possible.

If you are a spiritual person and creativity is spiritual, why don't you create more often? Perhaps it is because creativity is more of a battle than you anticipated? I hope I have helped you identify some of the enemies of your creativity, and I further hope you will determine to enter into a season of creativity that begins just as soon as you finish reading this chapter. Fight the good fight to be able to express your innate creativity that is latent within your heart and mind.

Your Choice

I have shared how fear hinders your creativity. We have seen how Adam's creativity was given and directed by God, and how Adam's sin resulted in fear, shame, and embarrassment that caused he and Eve to hide behind fig leaves and a bush when God came calling. Before Adam fell, he named the animals that God brought to him and, while the Fall did not eradicate Adam's creativity, the Fall tainted his creativity with sin. It has been that way ever since.

As we close out our discussion of this second Gold Mine Principle, you have three choices where creativity is concerned. I urge you to consider these options and then choose wisely the path that is God's will for you.

OPTION 1: You can refuse to be creative.

That doesn't mean that God doesn't love you; He does. That doesn't mean You are not saved. You are if you put your faith in Christ. You can, however, simply flat out refuse to confront your fear and release your creativity. The interesting thing is that you can't help but be creative, when you consider your ability to talk, reason, manage time, have children, start businesses, and the like.

Yet even while doing all that, you can refuse to use your creativity to express your purpose as Adam and Eve were commanded to do in the Garden: "God blessed them and said to them, 'Be fruitful and increase in number; fill the earth and subdue it. Rule over the fish in the sea and the birds in the sky and over every living creature that moves on the ground'" (Genesis 1:28). You can refuse to accept your mandate to be fruitful and rule, all the while maintaining a relationship with the Lord through prayer, reading and daily service.

OPTION 2: You can use your creativity for your own ends.

This is a subtle (or not-so-subtle) form of rebellion that tries to maintain control over creativity. Someone who doesn't know the Lord is generally in this condition, for they take what God has placed in them but then use it for selfish or self-willed purposes. Anyone who produces vulgar art, crude poetry, or obscene films, just to name a few examples, is taking their God-given creativity and using it for ungodly means. Now a refusal to be creative as outlined in option one is a form of rebellion, but this option two actively seeks to use creativity for *anything* besides godly purposes.

A good example of this kind of creative rebellion is found in Genesis 10:8-10a: "Cush was the father of Nimrod, who became a mighty warrior on the earth. He was a mighty hunter before the Lord; that is why it is said, 'Like Nimrod, a mighty hunter before the Lord.' The first centers of his kingdom were Babylon . . ." Nimrod used his creativity to build his own kingdom, and Babylon always represents an earthly kingdom that was established and existed to oppose God's rule and kingdom on earth.

OPTION 3: You can bring your creativity under the Lordship of Christ.

Your third option is to surrender your will where your creativity is concerned to God's will and plan for your life. When you do this, you confront your fears, put aside your concern for what others think, and do what is in your heart to do. When you do this, you accept the fact that Jesus came not just to reconcile your spiritual life to God, He came to reconcile all of you to God: " . . . and through him *to reconcile to himself all things*, whether things on earth or things in heaven, by making peace through his blood, shed on the cross" (Colossians 1:20 emphasis added).

Clearly then, options one and two are "sin," which is a word that simply means "missing the mark." When you avoid or trash your creative urges, you are missing the mark for your life, falling short of God's best for you. Generally, option one is where many Christians live and it is not an open or evil refusal to create, it is simply allowing fear to provide rational reasons why now is not the right time to write, travel, learn new languages, go back to school, or sing. While those reasons may seem rock solid, they are exposed by what you know to be true: With God, all things are possible.

P.S. Tell Your Story Creatively

I know that I promised that we were finished, but there is just one more piece to add to our theology of creativity, one more perspective that I hope will convince you the time to create is now and the materials to use as you create are your own ideas and impressions that stem from your life experience and creative gifts. I was studying and writing recently when I noticed a verse in Psalm 105:7 and it caught my attention. It's a verse you are probably familiar with, but what struck me is that the verse is an exhortation for you (and I) to publish and broadcast! You may not see it like that, but let me give you a little more background. Here is the verse: "Let the redeemed of the Lord tell their story—those he redeemed from the hand of the foe" (Psalm 107:2).

Do you have a story? I know you do, for God has done great things for you just as He has for me. That is what's known as your testimony and you are to tell it. One way is to do so in church, but in today's modern church services, where is there time to testify? That means you (and I) must find other ways to tell God's story, or your story in God. That is where publishing, social media, painting, sculpting, singing, song writing, and a host of other creative expressions enter the picture. For example, I seldom use social media for personal things, but I use it every day to publish what God is showing me and what I am learning. I do my best every day to tell my story. What about you?

After I noticed Psalm 107:2, I did a little more research and found two interesting things in Scripture that go along with that verse from Psalms. One is in Deuteronomy 31:19: "Now write down this song and teach it to the Israelites and have them sing it, so that it may be a witness for me against them." God instructed Moses to write a song and teach it to Israel. The theme of the song was to remind Israel of God's faithfulness in a day when they would go astray, but I had never noticed that God commanded Moses to be creative and write music. Do you have any music in you that needs to be written? That is another way of telling your story.

The second verse I found in my study was in Joshua 18:4:

"Appoint three men from each tribe. I will send them out to make a survey of the land and to write a description of it, according to the inheritance of each. Then they will return to me." I had never noticed before that God commanded the spies who were sent out to submit their report of what they saw in the Promised Land in writing. Their story was not what God had done but what God was going to do when they entered the Land He was giving them. Part of your story is your faith vision of what is yet to come.

So there you have three reasons to publish, write, and create: 1) to tell your story of what God has done for you; 2) to remind you and others of God's faithfulness; 3) to report what you see pertaining to God's purpose and plan for you that is yet to be.

GOLD MINE PRINCIPLE #3

GOAL SETTING

Be Careful Where You Dig

*"It is by his deeds that a lad distinguishes himself
if his conduct is pure and right."*
—— Proverbs 20:11 (NAS)

Chapter 12
Excellence Defined

Once you stake your claim to the field that holds your gold, it's important to begin digging in the correct area. It's not enough to know your purpose and be able to describe it to others. You must begin to achieve excellence in that purpose, which comes in part from setting and achieving goals.

We saw in Section One that the apostles chose to focus on their purpose and not be diverted by "waiting on tables." That allowed them to focus on the first Principle we discussed, which was purpose. The second result they achieved was excellence, for Acts 6:1-7 tells how the early church grew and prospered under their care. The simple decision to appoint deacons led to better care for the widows, growth in the church, and focused ministry for the apostles. The end result was excellence.

The verse used on the title page for this section (Proverbs 20:11) summarizes the two camps that believers generally fall into when it comes to defining excellence. The first is the "deeds" camp that would express excellence mainly in external things. They would build the finest buildings, publish the best ministry resources, and produce the most efficient ministry outreaches. The second is the "conduct" camp. They would point out that modern televangelists got into trouble not because they didn't have external excellence, but because they were missing an internal commitment to excellence that is expressed in holy living.

Unfortunately, both camps fall short of giving an accurate definition of excellence. The "deeds" people have not always been strong on behavior and therefore have sometimes discredited themselves through moral or integrity failures. In their pursuit of the goal, they often believe that the end justifies the means. On the other hand, the "conduct" people, although living a holy life, have often produced works that were shoddy and unimpressive by anyone's standards—if they produced any fruit or work at all!

As we begin this section, it's important for us to understand what excellence is and what it isn't. Years ago I set my goal as perfection, equating perfection with excellence. That brought me nothing but frustration, for I could never quite get it all right. No matter how well I planned or how hard I worked, something would go wrong. In time, the Lord helped me see the difference between perfection, which will never be achieved this side of eternity, and excellence, which is a heart attitude that produces quality work and conduct.

There are several situations that the Lord used to help me distinguish between perfection and excellence. One such instance was an event I was organizing in my early days as a meeting planner. I had responsibility for a small conference, including the program and publicity. After the program was finalized, I designed the promotional brochure and was ready to mail it when, to my dismay, I saw a misspelled word on the front cover!

The mailing labels were ready—the brochure needed to be in the mail yesterday—and I was confronted with an error that was clearly my fault since I was the only one who had proofed the brochure prior to printing. What was I to do? I was committed to excellence, but a new brochure would cost almost $400 to print, and my deadline was at hand.

I decided to reprint the brochure at my own expense. If it had gone out and I had not noticed the error, that would have been one thing. But the fact that I saw the error meant that I could not just send it out and trust those who saw it to overlook it and forgive my mistake. In this case, my commitment to excellence had to be more than good intentions.

Another time I was helping a friend put in a pool deck for

another member of our church. When we were planning the job, we estimated how much concrete we would need and then ordered some extra. To our shock, after we had poured what we ordered, we were two yards short! When the additional concrete came, it didn't match what had been put in previously.

The home owner wasn't pleased, but we hoped that he would overlook the mistake and not make us redo the job. After all, we were brothers in the Lord and friends, and mistakes do happen. He wasn't going to settle for a job that was unsatisfactory, however, and we ended up covering the deck with outdoor carpet at our expense. We were committed to excellence, and that commitment required that the job be finished according to the reasonable expectations of the one who was paying the bill. Asking his forgiveness wasn't an acceptable resolution to a job that had been inadequately planned and completed.

The third instance was when my wife and I reexamined our commitment to excellence as it pertained to having guests in our home. We weren't comfortable with our guests staying in our guest bedroom, which required that they share the bathroom at the far end of the hall with our children. So we decided to stay in the guest room ourselves and let our guests use our bedroom with its attached bath. It was easy to talk about excellence, but because we had a lot of visitors come through our home, it was more difficult to put it into practice.

And finally, my concept of excellence would not be complete without this last story. In 1986, my family and I visited the San Francisco area for a much-needed Christmas vacation. While there, we visited a mall where I purchased four dress shirts on sale at a Nordstrom's department store, well-known for its commitment to excellence. We visited several other stores when I suddenly realized that the bag with the shirts was missing! We retraced our steps and gradually realized that my shirts were nowhere to be found. As a last resort, I went to the counter where I had purchased the shirts and asked if anyone had turned in my bag to them.

Without hesitation, the salesperson told me to pick out

four more shirts. I explained that I couldn't afford four more shirts, to which she replied, "You won't have to pay for them!" She enlisted the help of two other employees, who cheerfully found four shirts like the ones that I had misplaced. I was in shock as she handed me the bag and wished me, "Happy New Year from Nordstrom's."

That's the kind of excellence that I want to practice as a follower of Jesus. Jesus' own ministry represents the epitome of excellence, for Mark 7:37 says, "People were overwhelmed with amazement. 'He [Jesus] has done all things well,' they said. 'He even makes the deaf hear and the mute speak.'" Not only did He do the right things at the right time, but He also did them well.

The word translated "well" in that verse is the Greek word, *kalos*, meaning "excellence, so that there is no room for blame." Jesus did what He did with the right heart and motives, and He produced excellence in His ministry. He was representing God, and His attitude and spirit communicated excellence through what He was and did. For Jesus, excellence did start within Him, yet wasn't complete until it found expression in His external actions.

The people in Jesus' day weren't used to a standard of excellence from their religious leaders. They knew that the Pharisees and lawyers taught but didn't always practice the truth. When Jesus came along and didn't just preach healing but also performed it with compassion and without condemnation, they were amazed. The world still tends to be amazed when they see true excellence in the Church.

That word *kalos* is used in several other verses of the New Testament: A man being considered for the office of elder "must manage his own family well [*kalos*]" (1 Timothy 3:4); "The elders who direct the affairs of the church well [*kalos*] are worthy of double honor" (1 Timothy 5:17); and "If you really keep the royal law found in Scripture, 'Love your neighbor as yourself,' you are doing right [*kalos*]" (James 2:8).

There's another Greek word that denotes excellence and that is *arete*. It's found in 2 Peter 1:5, which states, "Now for this very reason also, applying all diligence, in your faith supply moral *excellence* [*arete*]" (NAS, emphasis added). It simply refers to any particular moral excellence, whether it be honesty, patience, generosity, or similar traits. These traits are internal and begin in the heart.

The final verse to consider as we define excellence is found in 3 John 6: "You will do well [*kalos*] to send them on their way in a manner worthy of God." John was exhorting the brethren to offer excellent hospitality and care for visiting ministers. He described this excellent care as hospitality worthy of God.

For our discussion, therefore, we will define excellence as *doing all you do from a right heart and in a manner worthy of God.* This definition combines the concepts found in both *kalos* and *arete*, which are both external (actions) and internal (the heart).

Excellence is nothing less than work that is worthy of the God for whom it is done and that comes from a heart motivation of moral excellence that is the direct opposite of pride, arrogance, vanity, or greed.

This definition of excellence, which refers to both an internal and external expression, is what Covey referred to as the "inside-out-side" approach to life:

> The inside-outside approach [to life] says that private victories precede public victories, that making and keeping promises to ourselves precedes making and keeping promises to others. It says it is futile to put personality ahead of character, to try to improve relationships with others before improving ourselves.[1]

Excellence can't be contrived or a fad that a business, ministry, or person decides to pursue. It must be a lifestyle that begins in the heart and flows from there into work, and community and family action consistent with that heart condition.

Paul instructed the Colossians concerning excellence when he wrote, "Whatever you do, work at it with all your heart as working for the Lord, not for men, since you know that you will receive an inheritance from the Lord as a reward"

(Colossians 3:23-24). Paul wanted them to do everything with a right heart and not just to be noticed by men. But he also wanted them to work hard so that the visible results would give glory to the God who is worthy of all glory.

I have learned that excellence isn't inordinate attention to detail, as I had once thought. Rather it's a heart attitude that desires to give God the very best in every life situation. You raise your children with excellence because God cares for His children with excellence. Because God deserves your best efforts, you pursue excellence in your business, home, and ministry. This philosophy causes you to carry out even the smallest tasks with all your heart because you serve the Lord, whose very name is excellent. Out of this heart attitude, you create an atmosphere of excellence where even mistakes can't take away from the finished product because it was done in a manner worthy of God.

In the pursuit of excellence, however, sincerity isn't enough. The fact that you will never achieve perfection doesn't excuse sloppy work. You can be sincere and find yourself sincerely doing the wrong thing or sincerely doing things in a wrong way. You may even have a pure and tender heart toward the Lord and His service, sincerely doing good things for God. But excellence doesn't come from good intentions or being nice. It comes from a concerted effort that will settle for nothing less than the very best in every situation.

Ask yourself: "Am I producing work worthy of God? Does what I'm doing reflect excellence or just my best efforts under the circumstances? Do I settle for good instead of the best?" It's only when you abandon "the good" to give yourself to produce "the best" that you can truly produce excellence and glorify God.

It's a bit surprising that Israel didn't comprehend the issue of ministry excellence, for the Old Testament certainly tried to create the proper mindset in God's people for it. For example, Moses, David, and Solomon strictly adhered to the building plans God gave them for the tabernacle and the temple that they built using only the best materials. Furthermore, the sacrificial system, decreed by the Law, required that the animals being offered were to be without blemish—the best of the flock. The other offerings for the priests and Levites were to be "all the finest olive oil and all the finest new wine and grain they give the Lord as the firstfruits of their harvest" (Numbers 18:12). In short, the people were taught to give the Lord the best work of their hands.

Jeremiah wrote, "A curse [be] on him who is lax in doing the Lord's work" (Jeremiah 48:10). A "laid-back" attitude in working for God was not to be tolerated. Malachi rebuked the priests for the haphazard manner in which they carried out the work of the Lord:

> "A son honors his father, and a servant his master. If I am a father, where is the honor due me? If I am a master, where is the respect due me?" says the Lord Almighty. "It is you, O priests, who despise my name. But you ask, 'How have we shown contempt for your name?' You place defiled food on my altar. But you ask, 'How have we defiled you?' By saying that the Lord's table is contemptible. When you bring blind animals for sacrifice, is that not wrong? When you sacrifice crippled or diseased animals, is that not wrong? Try offering them to your governor! Would he be pleased with you?" says the Lord Almighty (Malachi 1:6-8).

Through the prophet, the Lord rebuked His people because they did not strive for excellence. They were approaching the things of God with a mentality of cutting corners instead of asking how they could present the finest service and offerings possible.

Perhaps the most powerful example of excellence in the Old Testament is found in 1 Kings 10:4-9:

> When the queen of Sheba saw all the wisdom of Solomon and the palace he had built, the food on his table, the seating of his officials, the attending servants in their robes, his cupbearers, and the burnt offerings he made at the temple of the Lord, she was overwhelmed. She said to the king,

"The report I heard in my own country about your achievements and your wisdom is true. But I did not believe these things until I came and saw with my own eyes. Indeed, not even half was told me; in wisdom and wealth you have far exceeded the report I heard. How happy your men must be! How happy your officials, who continually stand before you and hear your wisdom! Praise be to the Lord your God, who has delighted in you and placed you on the throne of Israel. Because of the Lord's eternal love for Israel, he has made you king, to maintain justice and righteousness."

The Queen of Sheba was overwhelmed by Solomon. She beheld not only excellence in action, but a happiness that was equally impressive. This pagan queen broke into praise ("Praise be to the Lord your God") when she described what she had seen. When was the last time anyone began praising God when they described the quality of your work, family, or ministry?

In the tradition of excellent ministry handed down to me by Solomon, Jesus, and many others, I want my brochures, websites, blog posts, emails, sermons, and work in general to represent the excellence of Him who called me out of darkness into His marvelous light. I want to express my creativity by working to make it the best it can be, not comparing my results to those of another—unless I am looking at theirs to see how I can improve mine. I am not perfect, nor are the things I work on perfect, but I can pursue excellence with all my heart and with a proper attitude.

Gold Nugget #11

"Do you see a man skilled in his work?
He will serve before kings; he will not
stand before obscure men."
—Proverbs 22:29

Martin Luther King captured this spirit when he once said, "If a man is called to be a street sweeper he should sweep streets even as Michelangelo painted, or Beethoven wrote music, or Shakespeare wrote poetry. He should sweep streets so well that all the hosts of heaven and earth will say, 'Here lived a great street sweeper who did his job well.'"

God has put the pursuit of excellence in you. William Temple, who served as Archbishop of Canterbury during World War II, spoke to that fact, saying, "At the root of all your being, your intellectual studies, the games you play, whatever it is, the impulse to do them well is and ought to be understood as being an impulse towards God, the source of all that is excellent." Amen and amen.

Let's now turn to a discussion of how you can pursue excellence on an ongoing basis.

Chapter 13

A Bull's-Eye
on Every Tree

I heard a story of a man who was walking toward a certain town in a day when men walked as a means of transportation. As he was walking, he took notice of targets painted on trees, fence posts, and barns. Each target had a bullet hole exactly in the middle—a bull's-eye on every one. He was impressed with the marksmanship and determined to find and meet this marksman as soon as he reached the town.

When he found him, the first question he asked the man was how had he become such an amazingly accurate shot. To his surprise, the man informed him that he wasn't a marksman at all. He just shot first and *then* painted the target around wherever his shot landed!

That's how we live when we don't set any goals. Going through life like that so-called marksman doesn't reflect excellence. We shoot first and make it look like we planned where it hit, but that's not the way to excellence. The highway to excellence doesn't involve following the path of least resistance for, as one man said, that "serves only to make both men and rivers crooked." The path of least resistance may make you look good and keep you from failure, but if you aim at nothing, you're sure to hit it. If you set no goals, you can't achieve any measure of excellence, and your purpose and creativity will languish.

Let's consider another example, this time from the world

of sports. I live in Pittsburgh, and I am an avid hockey fan. I never played hockey, but I go to as many games as possible. I'd go to the game early because I enjoyed the warm-ups. I watched as the teams came out to skate and check out the ice. The players would skate and shoot the puck at the goalie, who was wearing about 100 pounds of equipment, including big, heavy, leather leggings.

Although I sit high up in the upper deck seats, I could still clearly hear the big "whap" as the players would hit the goalie on those leggings with their sticks for good luck. All during the warm-ups, they would hit them—whap, whap, whap. As the game approached, the teams would take one final break to go to their locker rooms, only to return to do more "whapping." After the national anthem, the game would begin as the referee dropped the puck for a face-off at center ice.

Now picture in your mind the referee dropping the puck and one of the players passing to his teammate. See that player racing down the ice and shooting the puck at the opposing goalie. Visualize the puck getting past the goalie. The crowd stands, the players look, but alas, the referee forgot to put out the goal net! No one would know whether that shot had reached its goal or not. The game, with all its excitement and pre-game warm-ups, would have no meaning because no one would be able to determine whether that player or the goalie had achieved the goals to which they were dedicated. There would be no excellence achieved for the goalie or the shooter, because there were no set goals.

This hockey scenario reminds me of how it is sometimes in the body of Christ. We have big arenas that seat thousands, and people arrive early to get a good seat. Staff are running around warming up and making a lot of noise, sort of like the "whapping" noise of the players hitting the goalie. We play the game, but seldom know whether we have hit or missed the mark.

We then cover ourselves by saying, "We just want whatever size church God wants; we're not into numbers," or "If one person was helped, it was all worth it." We have no goals for Sunday School, attendance, or finances. We shoot and then paint a target around where the shot landed. There are no goals, and therefore less meaning to the event.

We can carry this same mentality into our homes and businesses. Because there are so many variables, we hedge on trying to estimate what our income will be, where and when we will go on vacation, and how many employees we will have next year at this time. We hesitate to set a goal for furthering our education or getting a new car because we may not make our goal.

Life has meaning when goals are established, and true excellence is achieved only when we set high goals. Without those lofty goals, you will stay in the comfort zone of life. With goals, you can begin to do "immeasurably more than all we ask or imagine, according to his power that is at work in us" (Ephesians 3:20).

One man who did accomplish "immeasurably more" was George Washington Carver. Carver was an African American scientist who lived and worked right after the Civil War, perhaps the worst time for a black leader to emerge in the war-torn and racially-divided South. Carver was a believer, however, who almost single-handedly improved the lot of the Southern farmer. In a time when his people had few opportunities, he excelled. How was Carver able to do this? He did it by serving his God and setting high goals.

Early in his career, Carver urged farmers to plant peanuts. When the first crop came in, however, there was no market for all those peanuts! Carver was crushed by his sense of failure and naivete. A fictional autobiography of Carver, drawing on true stories from his life, picks up the story from that point:

> I retreated into my lab, only there could I avoid the faces of my students and friends, only there could I be alone. But, somehow I knew I was not alone, even in the silence and stillness, I felt another presence. Falling to my knees, I begged forgiveness from my saviour and creator. And as I prayed, I was drawn

to my feet, out of the lab I went into the nearby woodlands and fields. The sun warmed my skin, the soft breezes refreshed my body. "Oh Mr. Creator", I asked softly, "Why did you make this universe?" The winds stirred the trees a bit, "Your little mind asks too much", came the answer. "Ask something more your size." Confused, I rubbed my chin. "What was man made for?" I whispered. Once more I seemed to hear a voice in the wind, "You are still asking too much little man. Try once more." I fell to my knees, "Mr. Creator, why did you make the peanut?" Once more the winds rustled through the trees, "Now you are asking questions your own size. Together, we will find the answers."[2]

George Washington Carver first set a goal of finding as many uses for the peanut as quickly as he could. From his experiments, he discovered more than 300 uses for the peanut. He not only discovered peanut butter and peanut oil, but also found ways to make paper, paint, and paste from that little nut. (In that same lab, Carver later discovered more than 100 uses for the sweet potato.) In a short time, peanut farmers could barely meet the public's demand for their crop!

At first, Carver had declared goals that were vague and unattainable, wanting to understand the universe and God Himself. But when he set his sights on a goal within his grasp, with the help of the Lord, he found himself on the highway that leads to excellence. Carver changed the world of agriculture because he set a demanding goal that required God's help.

Recently, someone gave me a copy of a speech delivered to a group of Alcoa employees by Paul O'Neill, then a company vice president, who later became president and went on to serve as the U.S. Secretary of the Treasury. One statement he made caught my attention: "If your calendar is filled up with people who want to see you instead of people you want to see, you haven't got a chance of success."[3]

According to O'Neill, his employees needed to develop

their own "action agenda" and stop letting others set it for them if they wanted to be the very best at what they did. He was talking about an action agenda, but he was really talking about setting goals, and then making room for them in the everyday flow of business.

Covey makes this point well in his discussion of the first habit of effective people. He calls it "proactivity":

> It [proactivity] means more than merely taking initiative. It means that as human beings, we are responsible for our own lives. Our behavior is a function of our decisions, not our conditions. We can subordinate feelings to values. We have the initiative and responsibility to make things happen.[4]

In 1997, I took my first graduate course in seminary called systematic theology. I thoroughly enjoyed the course, but it brought me face-to-face with my theological ignorance. I determined to do something about my lack of ministerial education, even though I had neither the money nor the time.

I set a goal then and there to earn my doctorate within an eight-year period. By so doing, I would graduate when my son graduated from high school. I had no idea where the time and money would come from, but it was something I wanted and needed to do. Furthermore, I believed that the Lord had put this goal in my heart.

I received my doctoral degree in pastoral ministry (I did it in those eight years), and people began to call me "Dr. John Stanko." All was well and good until 2005 when an investigative reporter, who was doing research on bogus graduate school degrees among ministers, sought me out to inform me that the school from which I graduated had not completed its accreditation. In a sense, my degree was worthless. What was my response?

In 2007, at the age of 57, I returned to an accredited institution and earned my Doctor of Ministry in 2011. I could not allow that bogus degree to hinder any opportunity the Lord would give me in the future, so I went back to school. I used my doctoral project as the basis for a book entitled *Changing the Way We Do Church: 7 Steps to a Purposeful Reformation.*

As I pursued both degrees, a spiritual dynamic was released through my faith. The money was always there for tuition, and the time to study and write papers somehow made itself available.

And speaking of my books, I started out in 1995 with this book as my first effort. I enjoyed it so much and the response was so exhilarating that I set a goal to write one book every year from that point forward. I missed a year or two, but by 2007, I had ten books. As I grew in faith and confidence, I wondered why I had limited myself to one book every year. I further wondered what my potential was to publish, and decided to set a more ambitious goal. As of this writing, I have 28 books, having done 18 books in 9 years. What's more, I started a publishing company and in the last two years, I have edited and helped publish 15 books for other people!

Can you see how goal-setting enhanced my purpose and released my creativity? Do you see how my doctoral studies added an important aspect to my preaching, to writing, and to my life in general? If I had only talked about getting more schooling or taking a few courses, I would have stopped short of all I could be and do. When I set the goal first and then let it be known that this was my intention with God's help, the finances, time, and everything else I needed were released. I've become better in all I do because I'm better equipped, leading to a higher degree of ministry excellence.

Gold Nugget #12

"All hard work brings a profit, but mere talk leads only to poverty."
—Proverbs 14:23

Maybe that power to achieve excellence lies in the commitment that you make to do something when a goal is set. W. H. Murray wrote these words about commitment:

Until one is committed there is hesitancy, the chance to draw back, always ineffectiveness. Concerning all acts of initiative there is one elementary truth, the ignorance of which kills countless ideas and splendid plans, that the moment one definitely commits oneself, providence moves too. All sorts of things occur to help one that otherwise would not have occurred. All stream of events issues from the decision, raising in one's favor all manner of unforeseen incidents and meetings and material assistance which no man could dream would come his way. I have learned a deep respect for one of Goethe's couplets:

> Are you in earnest? Seize this very minute.
> Whatever you do or dream you can begin it.
> Boldness has genius, power and magic in it.
> Only engage and then the mind grows heated,
> Begin and the work will be completed.

When you get on the highway to excellence and burn your bridges of doubt and worry behind you, the excitement begins. The apostle Paul understood this principle and had a cutting edge in his ministry that helped turn the world upside down. Let's look at Paul and learn how you can release that same dynamic of excellence into your life, work, and ministry.

Chapter 14

The Anatomy of a Goal

━━━━━━━━━━━━━━━━━━

Before we go any further, let's define what a goal is. My definition of a goal is: *a vision of how it is before it is.* That makes a goal something that requires faith, which is the assurance of things unseen (Hebrews 11:1). We will look at faith more closely as the fifth Gold Mine Principle. While some may view goal-setting as being incompatible with spirituality, I see goals as totally consistent, since they require faith. And faith in the Lord always leads to excellent results.

Others claim they are not skilled at setting goals. Yet I always ask those same people if they pray. When they say that they do, I ask them if a prayer request isn't actually a goal. When you pray, you start out with how it is before it is and pray to see it come to pass. You see someone who doesn't know the Lord and you pray that they will come to know Him; you are visualizing a goal, applying your faith in prayer, and working to see it come to pass.

In a less spiritual sense, I then ask if they have ever had a shopping list when they go to the store. That is a goal of all they would like to bring home from their shopping expedition. How about a menu for a meal? That is a goal, and in all probability, the person sees the food on the table before they even start cooking, maybe while they are shopping. And what about Christmas or any other special occasion? I ask if they plan the day—what will happen, what games or activities will take place, and who will be invited. All those are basic goals, so for anyone to say that they are not skilled with goal-setting just doesn't understand what a goal is.

In fact, man is teleological in nature. That's a big word that simply means humans are built to pursue a goal and have a purpose. We are like missiles looking for our targets. In the absence of a goal, we will cease to have a reason to live, and the death toll among recently-retired people who have no plan for their retirement bears witness to that truth. If you don't have a goal, you will adopt a general goal, and that will be to make today as close as possible to yesterday. Your goal will be to maintain the status quo, which is why change is so difficult to embrace, for the change is interfering with the goal!

When I share all this with people, suddenly they see how comfortable they should be in setting goals that require faith in God's great power. And indeed those who achieve a standard of excellence are often those who know how to set goals, pray, and have faith, just as George Washington Carver did.

You could also say that a goal is *an end result to be achieved through dreaming, planning, and diligence.* That process motivates you to begin and keeps you going when things seem to be going poorly. I've often used my imagination to visualize a certain goal, and then tried to figure out an action plan to help me achieve what I "saw." That process has allowed me to stay focused on the end and achieve things that began as just dreams (including this book).

You are created in the image of God, making you an awesome creature. This visualization is not you deciding on your own what you are going to do. This is a cooperative effort between you and the Holy Spirit. For example, Joseph in the Old Testament had a vision of his family bowing down before him. He didn't decide one day that he would be the head. The Spirit of the Lord showed that to him. And it cost him quite a lot to see it fulfilled, as we will discuss later.

For further evidence that goal-setting is a spiritual

exercise, consider the Apostle Paul. You may think it strange to say that Paul had goals, but he did! He wasn't haphazardly spreading the Gospel. Rather he had a plan with specific strategies to accomplish what he did. Consider these verses written by Paul himself as proof of this point:

- Therefore I run in such a way as not without aim [a goal]; I box in such a way, as not beating the air (1 Corinthians 9:26 NAS).

- And thus I aspired [set a goal] to preach the gospel, not where Christ was already named, that I might not build upon another man's foundation (Romans 15:20 NAS).

- But the goal of our instruction is love from a pure heart and a good conscience and a sincere faith (1 Timothy 1:5 NAS).

- And for this purpose [goal] also I labor, striving according to His power, which mightily works within me (Colossians 1:29 NAS).

- Now after these things were finished, Paul purposed [set a goal] in the spirit to go to Jerusalem after he had passed through Macedonia (Acts 19:21 NAS).

It is Philippians 3:14 (NAS), however, that gives the biblical anatomy of a goal: "I press on toward the goal for the prize of the upward call of God in Christ Jesus." That verse gives us the simple anatomy of a goal. First, a goal introduces tension and opposition. That's why most people don't like goals. They probably feel like they have more than enough tension and opposition without inviting more. But Paul "pressed on," and that means that something must have been pressing against him. Given that fact, Paul had to press through what was pressing against him with greater force if he was going to get anywhere. He understood that a goal would help him do just that.

Jesus must have understood that as well because He "for the joy set before him endured the cross, scorning its shame, and sat down at the right hand of the throne of God" (Hebrews 12:2). The goal for Jesus was the seat at the right hand of God. To get there, He pressed through the Cross and its shame. If a goal did that for Jesus, it will do the same thing for you.

As already mentioned, one goal for me was my doctorate. At times everything in me wanted to watch television, but I knew I had class work to do. At other times, I wanted to buy a *Time* magazine in an airport so I could just do some leisurely reading. I couldn't do that because I had class reading to complete if I was going to finish my goal and pursue excellence. There was something pressing against me, and I had to press through it. The goal of my doctorate helped me to do that.

My goal of writing books is another example. Before I even write a book, I spend some time thinking about how I will sign the book for people who request an autograph. Then I see myself sitting at a table, signing that greeting in the book, and then handing it to a smiling customer. That vision and then the goal help me press through the busyness of life that tries to talk me out of finishing the task.

If you already have tension and opposition in your life without goals, why not set some goals of where you want to go? Then the pressure and opposition will have some meaning because they are coming to prevent you from getting where you want to go. Your desire to achieve your goal will give you incentive to overcome it all to succeed.

Second, Philippians 3:14 teaches that **a goal offers a prize**. When you set a goal, two things can happen: You can achieve it or fail trying. In the game of goal setting, there are winners and losers. That's part of life, but too often you can try to play it safe. There's no prize or excellence in living like that. If you set the goal, you may not win; if you don't set the goal, you can't win. There's a big difference.

Some spiritual people are uncomfortable with the concept of winning and losing. They don't want to play the game, so to speak, for it requires more effort, aggressiveness, and will power than they believe truly spiritual people should exert. They are more comfortable with allowing things to happen rather than helping to make things happen. Yet, success is never an accident, even for spiritual people. Goals give you focus and energy, and are an important part of your walk with the Lord.

Next, **a goal is upward**. It brings you closer to God and godliness (if it's truly a godly goal). Again, I draw from my experience of going back to school. My doctoral studies taught me a great love about the Lord and His word. That goal was not just academic; it was spiritual. And because it was, it brought me closer to the Lord and gave me greater love for Him, His people, and His Word. Almost any goal teaches you more about yourself and the Lord. It gives you a testimony when you achieve it, and causes you to pray and seek the Lord for answers and solutions to problems the goal brings.

And finally, **a goal involves a call**, a specific task that God has set before you to do. It's my belief that the Lord put the desire for my degree in my heart in the first place. What I accomplished was something that He had set before me to do. It was up to me to accomplish it with the creativity that I have developed and the gifts He has given me. Ephesians 2:10 is clear that God has laid out a course that we are to navigate by faith: "For we are God's handiwork, created in Christ Jesus to do good works, which God prepared in advance for us to do." I maintain that those good works will not get done haphazardly or without a plan. Once you identify the good works, you will only do them with proactive goals.

What's more, those good works are part of your potential, and you won't know what that potential is in its fullest expression when you start out. Your potential to write a book may be five or twenty-five books, and you won't know until you start writing. The point is that goals will help you discover and fulfill your potential, which may continue to expand as you are faithful to do what you can today.

Paul set goals that were prompted by the Spirit, and he helped turn the world upside down with the message of the Gospel. He didn't just run the race any way he chose. He set the course by establishing goals and then ran that course with discipline and purpose. Today many emulate Paul's method of ministry because it set such a high standard of effectiveness and excellence. Like Paul, who encountered struggles when he pursued his goals, you too will encounter any number of obstacles standing in your way as you seek to win the prize at the end of your goal.

In some sense, the ball is in your court. You can enjoy the presence and mercy of God, but God doesn't give you those things because He wants you to feel good. He wants you to bear fruit and do greater things than even Jesus did. Here are the words of Jesus explaining God's will where your fruit is concerned:

> "Very truly I tell you, whoever believes in me will do the works I have been doing, and they will do even greater things than these, because I am going to the Father. And I will do whatever you ask in my name, so that the Father may be glorified in the Son. You may ask me for anything in my name, and I will do it" (John 14:12-14).

> "I am the vine; you are the branches. If you remain in me and I in you, you will bear much fruit; apart from me you can do nothing. If you do not remain in me, you are like a branch that is thrown away and withers; such branches are picked up, thrown into the fire and burned. If you remain in me and my words remain in you, ask whatever you wish, and it will be done for you" (John 15:4-7).

> "You did not choose me, but I chose you and appointed you so that you might go and bear fruit— fruit that will last—and so that whatever you ask in my name the Father will give you" (John 15:16).

God is after something, and you are part of His plan. Don't receive His grace in vain. Use it rather to set high goals and count on that grace to help you creatively succeed with excellence. With that in mind, let's now turn to a discussion of those things that will work against you achieving your goals and how you can minimize their effect.

Chapter 15

Your Goals Have Enemies

There are four enemies that work against you setting or pursuing goals. They show up every time you think about or set a goal without fail. If you are aware of these enemies, you can recognize them, for often they disguise themselves and appear to be rational, reasonable excuses for why you cannot do what you would like to do. In some ways, they are consistent with the dilemma that Paul described to be present in his own life: "For I know that good itself does not dwell in me, that is, in my sinful nature. For I have the desire to do what is good, but I cannot carry it out. For I do not do the good I want to do, but the evil I do not want to do—this I keep on doing" (Romans 7:18-19). Let's look at the four enemies of your goals in more detail and then develop some strategies to help you avoid them.

Enemy #1: Unbelief

For the first few years when I pastored a small church, we had a terrible sound system. We had a pair of stereo speakers, cheap microphones, and we were content with that for much too long. The church fasted for three weeks one January, as was our custom. During that fast, I determined (and sensed it was God's will) that it was time for us to get a new and better system, so that became our goal. Shortly thereafter, we heard about a system for sale that had everything we needed. There was only one problem—our lack of money.

The church didn't have any savings, nor did we have many high-income members. Not letting that deter us, we told the man that we would buy his system. I then announced that a special offering would be taken two weeks later. That offering was a miracle. One man just happened to receive a surprise settlement from an insurance company, and he alone paid for half the system. I'm still not sure where the rest of the money came from, but we were able to pay for that system with cash. That goal helped us have better audio quality that contributed to our pursuit of ministry excellence.

Looking back, I can see that I put up with an inadequate sound system for two years because we had a small church, and I didn't believe God could give us anything more. That attitude represents the first and most formidable enemy working against your goals—**unbelief**. The writer of Hebrews tells us,

> Who were they who heard and rebelled? Were they not all those Moses led out of Egypt? And with whom was he angry for forty years? Was it not with those who sinned, whose bodies fell in the desert? And to whom did God swear that they would not enter his rest if not *to those who disobeyed*? So we see that they were not able to enter, *because of their unbelief* (Hebrews 3:16-19, emphasis added).

This passage equates unbelief and disobedience. If you're walking in unbelief, you're being disobedient, and that's sin, no matter how you slice it.

One time my family rented a house where we kept the trash cans in a small alcove outside the front door. One morning I went out to take the cans to the curb and as I did, I walked into a fairly substantial spider web that had been spun head high. That web acted like a hair net and stuck to my hair like glue. I went back inside and stood in front of mirror to get the web out of my hair and the thought came to me, "That's how unbelief is." You can walk into it and not even realize it until it's too late. It clings to you, and it requires some effort to get it off.

For instance, you may have the thought one day, "I need to learn Spanish." If you're not careful, you will immediately walk into the web of unbelief and think, "No, I can't. I don't have time. Besides, I was not good at languages in school. Maybe when my kids are in college, I'll have time to do it."

Or maybe you have the idea that you want to learn to play the piano. But then the web traps you with thinking like, "Oh, it's too late in life. I don't have the time or patience to practice." The web of unbelief comes on you and sticks to you like glue. You're paralyzed in that web and afraid to move out.

I'll give you another example of what I mean. I once owned a car that began to give me all kinds of trouble. After two or three major breakdowns, I was still determined to be a good steward and not buy another one. The problem was that I found myself witnessing to every tow truck driver within a 50-mile radius of where I lived. I told the Lord, "God, if you want me to witness to these men, please send them to my church and not to pick me up in my broken-down car!" But I was still determined to be a good steward.

Finally, I broke down in Perdido Key, Alabama, and had to be towed more than 85 miles back home. I had had enough. When I got home, I went to a Dodge dealer and said, "I want a Dodge Caravan." The salesman asked, "Which one?" and I responded, "I don't care, just give me your best deal." I signed on the bottom line and drove that van home.

I didn't have the money in my budget for either a down payment or the monthly payment of $429.52. I paid off that car early, however, and it was a tremendous blessing for over 120,000 miles. At first I didn't believe that the Lord could get me a new car. But then I decided that if I could have faith for the old one to run, I could have faith to be able to make the payments on a new one.

You may long for the latest technology gizmo, new musical equipment, or an advanced degree. Is $400 per month keeping you from something that could launch your career or ministry or make your current one more productive? Is that faith?

Life is a Gold Mine: 20th Anniversary Edition

If you are serious about excellence and there is something you need to help you achieve it, are you willing to use your faith to get it? Again, it's easy to talk about excellence but not always comfortable to pursue it.

It's not faith that requires you to know everything from the beginning before you'll step out and do something. It's presumption and pride to insist that the Lord show you everything before you will trust Him and take the first step. Didn't Abraham leave his country not knowing where he was going? Did God explain everything to him before he left? Of course he didn't, and so He commended Abraham for his faith and made him your father in the faith because Abraham heard God and acted. You are expected to follow in his footsteps.

Now you may think I'm teaching debt here, but I'm not. David described what I'm trying to impart when he wrote,

> For though the Lord is exalted, yet He regards the lowly; but the haughty He knows from afar. Though I walk in the midst of trouble, Thou wilt revive me; Thou wilt stretch forth Thy hand against the wrath of my enemies, and Thy right hand will save me. *The Lord will accomplish what concerns me*; Thy lovingkindness, O Lord, is everlasting (Psalm 138:6-9 NAS, emphasis added).

The bottom line is this: Do you believe that the Lord will accomplish what concerns you, regardless of how impossible it seems? If you don't, then you're walking in disobedience, because you are commanded to have faith. If you do believe that, then what are you prepared to do about it?

At one time I trusted the Lord for over $2 million in ministry income. I could do that in part because I learned to trust him for a $429 monthly van payment. We will return to the subject of faith in Section Five, but for now, let's end our discussion of unbelief with a poem:

> There's no thrill in easy sailing, when the skies are clear and blue. There's no joy in only doing things, which anyone can do. But there is some

114

satisfaction that is mighty sweet to take, When you reach a destination that you thought you'd never make.——Unknown

Setting goals in faith will help you go where you thought you never could. It will provide your greatest testimonies of how the Lord helped you to do the impossible as you trusted Him. If you pursue the right goals, they will add to your level of excellence, releasing your creativity and enabling you to fulfill your purpose.

Enemy #2: Low Self-Esteem

The next great enemy of your goals is low self-esteem. I respected and utilized principles of inner healing and deliverance in my pastoral counseling, but after 20 years of pastoral ministry, I've come to the conclusion that if you suffer from low self-esteem, you're really in a pretty good place. Now before you accuse me of error, let me explain what I mean.

Paul wrote in Romans 7:15, "What I want to do, I do not do," and as we saw in verse 18 above, "nothing good lives in me...for I have the desire to do what is good, but I cannot carry it out." Some think Paul was talking about his life before Christ when he wrote this, while others think he was stating a fact of life that was true even after conversion.

Paul was describing his true current condition when he wrote those verses. After all Paul had learned and done, he knew there wasn't anything in him that was "good." The same is true for you, if you'll stop and think about it. There's nothing in you that you can spit-shine and present to God that will be acceptable in His sight. Thank God that's not the end of the story, for He gave you the Holy Spirit as a downpayment of the glory that is yet to come. You didn't receive some portion or expression of the Holy Spirit, but rather the same Holy Spirit that raised a dead man (Jesus) back to life!

If you're feeling like you aren't worth much, you may be right! There may be no good thing in your flesh, but the Spirit in you has made and is making you into a new creation. Focus your worth on what the Spirit is building in you, and you'll have new vision for what you can accomplish through that partnership. You'll also realize that your ability to accomplish great things for the Lord doesn't depend on how your father treated you or how your mother changed your diapers.

Paul also wrote in Galatians 2:20 (NKJV), "I have been crucified with Christ, it is no longer I who live but Christ who lives in me, and the life I now live in the flesh, I live by faith in the son of God who loved me and gave himself for me." Now it may be difficult for you to think of Paul as dead and worthless. He went on to write, "I am the worst [of all sinners]" (1 Timothy 1:15). You may think Paul was just saying that in religious humility, but it was true. Paul was the worst. He was a murderer and thought he was doing God a favor by killing people. In essence, he was saying, "It is no longer I who live but Christ who lives with me, and I'm just as glad. Let Him shine through me and let me be the vessel He works through."

Gold Nugget #13

"The Lord will be your confidence."
—Proverbs 3:26

Paul also explained his ministry in terms of what God was doing in him:

> I became a servant of this gospel by the gift of God's grace given me through *the working of his power* . . . Now to him who is able to do immeasurably more than all we ask or imagine, according to his *power that is at work within us* (Ephesians 3:7, 20, emphasis added).

The phrases "working" and "at work" both come from the Greek word *energeia*, and it's the word from which we derive the word "energy." There was a divine energy in Paul that came from the Holy Spirit. Will it be any different for you? You won't do great and excellent things for God because you're smart, talented, or gifted. God will use those things, but you'll accomplish your goals.

Paul prayed for the Ephesians that they would know "his incomparably great power for us who believe. That power is like the working of his mighty strength" (Ephesians 1:19). You have power through faith. If you want power to do more with excellence, focus your faith on some high goals. Get your eyes off your inadequacies and on the greatness of the power. God will only do "immeasurably more than all we ask or imagine *according to his power that is at work in us*" (emphasis added). If there's no power working in you, then God can't do the immeasurably more. It's just that simple.

Enemy #3: Fear

The third enemy you have in goal setting is fear, which we discussed earlier as part of our Adamic nature. We inherited the fear syndrome from our first parents. You can be so paralyzed by the fear that you may not try to do anything at all, and that can include fear of failure, success, criticism, missing the Lord, poverty, injuries, loss of relationships, and death. This truth came home to me as I was reading the sports section one day.

When Pete Rose, former baseball great, was closing in on the record for the most career base hits, an interesting statistic caught my eye. Rose had more than 4,000 hits and had a career batting average of just over .300. That meant that he had come to bat more than 14,000 times. If he had 4,000 hits, that meant he had failed to get a hit more than 10,000 times! For every hit (his goal every time he stepped to the plate), he had 2.5 failures. Yet he was considered a great player until character flaws pulled him down.

Do your past failures or the fear of new ones tend to keep you in the dugout? For fear of striking out, will you not even try to get a hit? Are you so afraid you'll do the wrong thing that you miss opportunities to do the right thing? If you answered yes to any or all of those questions, then you have a problem with the fear of failure and you need to face it and get rid of it.

It may help you to realize that mistakes and failures are part of the learning process. You don't discipline a child learning to walk when that child falls down. Because they are learning, you encourage them to keep on trying. Pete Rose wasn't born knowing how to hit a baseball. It's the same with life and with goals, even spiritual ones.

People ask me every now and then how I learned to plan conferences. (This is another aspect of creating order out of chaos. When I begin planning a conference, there's nothing there; yet order comes from this void when I go to work.) Even though most of my conferences have gone smoothly, I've had my share of failures. Those failures have taught me more than my successes. If that is true, were those "failures" really failures or were they really successes that taught me important principles through difficult circumstances? Even a baseball player may strike out only to learn something about the pitcher that enables him to hit a home run the next time up to the plate. Suddenly his strikeout is not a failure, but a learning experience on the way to a success.

I planned a meeting in Dallas one time that was a disaster. The night before the event, I had a dream that the meeting was a disaster. Slipping into the bathroom at 3 AM in order not to awaken my roommate, I actually took notes, listing 14 things that went wrong with the meeting in my dreams.

When I awoke the next morning, I shared the dream with my coworkers. We were expecting 1,200 people, however, and didn't really take the dream too seriously until that evening when only 300 people came. It was a financial and spiritual disaster. It was painful, and I never want to have a meeting like that again. But I lived and learned through it (and you will, too) when you "fail."

Then there's the question that people always ask: "How can I be sure what I want to do is from the Lord?" My response is always the same: "How do you know it *isn't*?" You must learn to stop making (out of fear of failure and unbelief) the Lord prove that your idea is from Him and ask Him for proof that it isn't.

As added help in this matter, consider what Proverbs 16:3

says in the Amplified Version:

> Roll your works upon the Lord—commit and trust them wholly to Him; *He will cause your thoughts to be agreeable to His will*, and so shall your plans be established and succeed (emphasis added).

Isn't one goal of the Spirit to give you the mind of Christ? Can this happen, and you not even realize it? You can have the mind of Christ, and it occurs in a supernaturally natural manner. How do you expect it to happen—with lightning bolts and electric jolts? Stop dismissing your ideas as insignificant; they may be dripping with potential, waiting for you to accept and act on them.

You're still not convinced? Then consider what Luke wrote to open his Gospel: "*It seemed good also to me* to write an orderly account for you, most excellent Theophilus" (Luke 1:3, emphasis added). He didn't write that the Lord led him to write or that five prophets spoke a word for him to write. Rather he wrote, "It seemed good to me." Luke had a good idea that was supernaturally natural.

It was the Holy Spirit who prompted that idea, and it was part of Luke's purpose. Luke then expressed his creativity—the gospel was written with his vocabulary and from his perspective—and produced a work that has lasted for 2,000 years. The result was the word of God in Luke's Gospel! Your ideas and goals that come from having the mind of Christ are the keys to your success as you pursue excellence.

Look at the Holy Spirit-prompted goal that Jonathan set in 1 Samuel 14. King Saul and 600 men were camped "under a pomegranate tree in Migron" (1 Samuel 14:2). They were going through drills every day, acting like an army in every way except one— their enemies held the high places, and Saul wasn't attacking them. He was just playing soldier!

Jonathan, on the other hand, said to his armor-bearer, "Come, let's go over to the Philistine outpost on the other side" (1 Samuel 14:1). That was easier said than done. Jonathan had chosen a tough goal: "On each side of the pass that Jonathan intended to cross to reach the Philistine outpost was a cliff" (1

Samuel 14:4). Jonathan, however, was unfazed:

> Jonathan said to his young armor-bearer, "Come,
> let's go over to the outpost of these uncircumcised
> fellows. Perhaps the Lord will act in our behalf.
> Nothing can hinder the Lord from saving, whether
> by many or by few" (1 Samuel 14:6).

Jonathan wasn't looking for a way to dismiss his idea.
He wasn't asking God to prove it by sending a prophet or some
other miraculous messenger. Jonathan made it easy for the Lord
to confirm what he set out to do: "If they say to us, 'Wait there
until we come to you,' we will stay where we are and not go up to
them. But if they say, 'Come up to us,' we will climb up, because
that will be our sign that the Lord has given them into our hands"
(1 Samuel 14:9-10). What faith!

If I were the Philistines, I would of course call out to
Jonathan to come up. Why should I leave the advantage of
my high place? Yet Jonathan chose the natural response of his
enemies to confirm his goal. To him, it confirmed that they were
afraid and that he would have the element of surprise on his side.
He wasn't looking for a way out of the goal he had set, but rather
for a way in.

While the armies of God were marching around in the
valley, Jonathan was scaling the walls of his enemies. Who
had the standard of excellence—Saul who was drilling the army
in the valley or Jonathan who stepped out and actually brought
the victory? Maybe Saul wanted his army to be the best-drilled
army around, but that wasn't the key to excellence for an army
surrounded by its enemies! Perhaps Jonathan didn't do it as neatly
as Saul would have, but he knew how to set a goal that was high
and divinely inspired, and he wasn't afraid of failure.

When we discussed the concept of low self-esteem earlier, we saw that there is energy working in you through the Spirit.
Second Corinthians 6:1 adds to your understanding of this energy
when it refers to you as "God's fellow workers." The Greek word
for "fellow workers" is *sunergeia*, from which the word "synergy" is derived. Properly defined, synergy is "the cooperative

action of discrete agencies so that the total effect is greater than the sum of the two effects taken independently." Synergy means that one plus one equals three, or five, or ten!

Covey wrote that synergy is the sixth habit of effective people and is the synergy between people, a common place for it to occur. The synergy Paul described is between you and God! Imagine the power that is present when God is your "fellow worker"!

"You + God = synergy" of the highest order. He could accomplish His purpose without you but has chosen not to. You working with God can do more than just you alone. That working relationship can produce excellence because He who is excellent can reproduce His excellence through what you do.

The Bible teaches, "Five of you will chase a hundred, and a hundred of you will chase ten thousand" (Leviticus 26:8). Without synergy, two should only be able to put 40 to flight. But working together will increase the battle results of two people five-fold!

Paul calls you and me God's "fellow workers." Because of who you work with, you should dress and act like God's fellow worker. That fact doesn't depend on how you feel, where you've been, or how many failures you've had. Synergy can still be realized when you give yourself to the purpose and the goals of God.

Shake off the spirit of failure! Someone once said, "God is playing chess with man; He matches his every move." Move and watch God move with you. Another person said, "No one can ever be a complete failure, for he can then serve as a horrible example for someone else." Even if you fail, someone can point to you and say, "Don't ever grow up to be like that."

Before we move on, it may surprise you that I listed success as one of the fears in my list above. Most people don't see how they can be afraid of the very thing they believe they are pursuing, but they can. You may be afraid to start a business because it may grow beyond your ability to manage it—that's fear of success. You may not compose your first song or poem because you are not sure if you will be able to sustain your creative edge—that's fear of success. Any fear is insidious and seldom shows up as a ghost in the night hours; rather as I stated earlier, it's rational and seems to make sense. That's not true, for any and every fear is debilitating and ungodly, for God has not given us a spirit of fear (see 2 Timothy 1:7).

What's more, stop being surprised that you may be afraid. Expect it! Go looking for it! Don't be afraid to find the fear, for it's lurking somewhere, hiding behind a well-meaning or credible excuse.

Enemy #4: Lack of diligence

The final enemy we will discuss in this chapter is lack of diligence. You can easily underestimate what it will take to achieve your goal and sometimes you want to give up. When you say, "Lord, I want to be used by you," the Lord often responds, "Oh, really? Well, just sign this contract." When you study the contract, however, there's nothing on the page. The Lord then says, "Well, just sign it, and I'll fill in the terms later."

Gold Nugget #14

"A slothful man does not roast his prey, but the precious possession of a man is diligence."
—Proverbs 12:27 (NAS)

That is what the Lord did in my own call to ministry. I waited 16 years for a pulpit. I was called to the ministry when I was seven years old; when I met the Lord at age 23, He confirmed my call. Five years later, I moved to Mobile, Alabama, where I preached two times in 11 years! I was one of the youngest men on a 20-man pastoral ministry team. There I was, praying for 19 men ahead of me to "go home" or get transferred so that I could have a chance to minister!

During those long years, however, I used Covey's second habit—begin with the end in mind—to help me prepare myself. I wanted people to remember me as a great preacher (I still have a ways to go on that), so I started preparing to be a great preacher.

During those 11 years, I planned, prepared, and dreamed for the day when I would get a pulpit.

I would analyze sermons and see what worked and what didn't. I would preach to myself, my kids, the goldfish, my home meeting, and to anybody who would listen. At the same time, the Lord worked some of the character in me that would be needed for the ministry to which I was called. When eventually I went to Orlando to pastor, I was ready because I had been diligent. I will discuss my call to the ministry again in Section Five.

There's even a better example in the Old Testament of what I am trying to communicate. Earlier in this section, I mentioned that in the book of Genesis, Joseph had two dreams, both indicating that his family would bow down to him. Joseph was 17 years old when he had those dreams. Shortly thereafter, his brothers sold him into slavery. When he arrived in Egypt, Joseph faithfully served as a servant in Potiphar's house. Mrs. Potiphar tried to seduce Joseph, but when he didn't succumb to her advances, she lied and claimed that he tried to seduce her. That landed Joseph in jail.

When he was 30 years old, or about 13 years after his dreams, Joseph was brought before Pharaoh and interpreted Pharaoh's dreams. Pharaoh was so impressed that he promoted Joseph to be his second in command, but the story didn't end there. Joseph needed to be more diligent before the dream or goal would come to pass.

Joseph then led Egypt through seven years of plenty. By then, he was 37 years old and there was still no sign that his dreams would ever be fulfilled. It wasn't until the second year of the famine (see Genesis 45:6) that Joseph revealed himself to his brothers. Just prior to that, we are told that Joseph "remembered his dreams about them" (Genesis 42:9).

If you have trouble remembering your dreams from last night, how did Joseph manage to keep his dreams alive for at least 22 years? He kept them fresh in his mind by rehearsing them. Even though everything seemed to work against his dreams coming to pass, Joseph was diligent in jail, in Potiphar's house, and as Pharaoh's vice president. Joseph knew how to keep the goal out in front of him! He maintained a standard of excellence no matter what he was doing, and it led to his promotion and the fulfillment of the dreams the Lord had given him.

I have tried to be diligent in my pursuit of purpose and creativity. That has caused me to write 790 weekly letters called *The Monday Memo* and give them away. It caused me to write a daily devotional and give it away through Facebook, Twitter, LinkedIn, and my own personal blog. I wrote a weekly Bible study for nine years that enabled me to write a devotional for every verse in the New Testament. I have written 28 books. You get the idea—I hope. You will work to achieve your goals, but it will be fun and God will be with you.

The lesson for you is to be diligent. Use the time you have now to prepare for the day when you will attain your goal. If you'll keep your goal in front of you, regardless of what the circumstances look like, you'll be motivated to produce excellence, even if what you're doing seems totally unrelated to the goal you're pursuing.

I urge you to face the enemies of your goals and learn to master them. Deal with the web of unbelief. Shrug off low self-esteem. Face the truth, recognize your fears, and don't allow them to stop you in your tracks. And apply the necessary diligence to see what you've started come to a successful conclusion. If you're willing to do all this, then proceed to the next chapter, which will lead you in an exercise to help formulate and write down your goals.

Chapter 16

Let's Set Some Goals

As we begin this chapter, let's look at Habakkuk 2:1-5:

> I will stand at my watch and station myself on the ramparts; I will look to see what he will say to me, and what answer I am to give to this complaint. Then the Lord replied: "Write down the revelation and make it plain on tablets so that a herald may run with it. For the revelation awaits an appointed time; it speaks of the end and will not prove false. Though it linger, wait for it; it will certainly come and will not delay."

From this passage, you have the basic steps of how to set your own goals. Let's look at it phrase by phrase.

1. *I will stand at my watch and station myself on the ramparts.* First of all, get away from the phone and all other distractions. Go to the library, a public park, your church sanctuary, or your favorite place of prayer. If you're really serious, you may want to fast and pray before you begin or during the process.

Then "station yourself on the ramparts." Get above the situation in which you're now living. Forget about money (or the lack of it), education, your current job, or the lack of ministry opportnities or career advancements. Remember that "God raised us up with Christ and seated us with him in the heavenly realms in Christ Jesus" (Ephesians 2:6). Take your place with Christ and look down on your life.

Exercising faith that "in his heart a man plans his course, but the Lord determines his steps" (Proverbs 16:9), begin to examine every area of your life. Ask yourself where you want to be and what you would like to accomplish in the next two years in your job, ministry, family, finances, health, and spiritual life. As you formulate goals, ask yourself what you must do to make those goals a reality.

For instance, if you are a pastor and desire to see your church double in size within two years, what is your plan to see that happen? How often will you pray? What will you preach? And who will you enlist to help reach your goal? If you want to write a book, how many pages per day or week must you write to be done in two years? If you want or need to do more reading, how many books will you read per month and what kind of books will they be?

2. *I will look to see what he will say to me.* Add to your goals those that may be unexpected or seem out of character for you because they may be from the Lord. You may never have thought of furthering your education, but sense that may be an issue about which the Lord is speaking. If it is, make it a goal. Remember not to dismiss something right away as being ridiculous or far-fetched. Exercise some faith and do something to see if the Lord won't confirm your unexpected thoughts and desires.

Take time also to renew those past dreams that you've abandoned due to family responsibilities, lack of time or money, or discouragement. Let the Lord energize those old "castaways" into active goals once again.

I can't emphasize enough the need for you to take your impressions and thoughts seriously during this process. Don't be too quick to dismiss them as wild or impossible. At the same time, a goal that you will kick the winning goal in the next World Cup when you are 52 and not in great shape is actually a goal based in fear! You are so afraid that you cannot do what's in your heart that you will choose something ridiculous that you cannot possibly achieve. In all probability, your biggest stretch goals have been in your heart for a long time, but fear has not allowed you to embrace them as doable or possible, so you conveniently circumvent or ignore them. See what God will say to you and find a way to do it instead of finding excuses not to—or choosing impossible scenarios.

3. *Write down the revelation.* Don't just think about your goals; write them down! And don't just write them down on a scrap of paper or a legal pad that can be misplaced easily. Record your goals in something you carry with you everywhere. That is certainly easier to do than when I first wrote this book in 1995. I am sure you have a mobile device that would be a perfect carrier of your goal list. The whole idea is to keep your goals before you so that you cannot ignore them.

In Psalm 50:17, the Lord rebuked His people, "You hate my instruction and cast my words behind you." When you have a goal and you believe it's something that the Lord has put in you to do, don't cast those words behind you. Keep them in front of you. Writing them down helps you do that. Writing down goals also helps ensure that you take them seriously. Furthermore, it prevents you from abandoning those goals during tough times.

4. *For the revelation awaits an appointed time.* A goal isn't truly a goal until a time schedule has been worked out for its fulfillment. Once you have answered what you will do, you must then decide when you expect to complete it. Until that happens, a goal still lives in the land of dreams.

Having said that, I want to put some limitations on that. If your goal is to lose 25 pounds, and it's January, and you set the achievement date to be December 31, that's not a timely goal. That's procrastination, for you will say to yourself in February, "I have 10 months," and in April, "I still have eight months." In a sense, all your goals are *now* goals that need to be pursued *now* and achieved as soon as possible. Don't use your end dates to create avoidant behavior. Use them to create urgency!

As mentioned previously, Nehemiah was asked by his boss, the king, "How long will your journey take, and when will you get back?" Nehemiah responded, "It pleased the king to send me, so I set a time" (Nehemiah 2:6). Nehemiah had not even seen Jerusalem or the scope of the task, but he set a timetable as best he could.

Robert Schuller, a one-time famous televangelist, once wrote,

> When you set goals, put a time limit on them. Without it you are normally and naturally lazy and lethargic more often than you want to admit. It's amazing how much you can accomplish in a short period of time if the pressure is on. What do you do when you have not succeeded in meeting your time limit, and it becomes apparent that the project will take longer than you expected? You keep walking in faith. *You revise your timetable*: "It's not impossible, it just takes a little longer." Suddenly seemingly unachievable projects become very realistic! What can you accomplish if you take ten years? You might be able to get a new degree. Perhaps you can acquire a much larger financial base. You might even be able to overcome that handicap. Keep walking the walk of faith. *Don't give up believing; just revise the timetable!* God never promised to deliver an answer to prayer according to our timetables (emphasis added).[5]

Once you have set a time limit, you are ready for the next step.

5. *Though it lingers, wait for it.* Schuller spoke of the need for flexibility in the above quote, and he's right. Goal setting is not a science but an art. You don't have perfect knowledge, and you can't foresee the unexpected. If you could, you may not set out on your goal's journey at all! You make your best estimates, realizing that you may need more time.

Schuller also wrote,

> Give God time, and He will perform the miracle. When a human condition appears to be totally impossible, don't check out; ask for an extension of time. The hotel sign reads, "Check out time is 12:00 noon." Don't believe it if you run into a predicament! Ask and believe. They will extend the check out time. Just don't get locked into an iron-clad schedule.

Don't surrender leadership to a clock or a calendar. Of course you set time-dated goals. Of course you generate energy by creating urgency. But be prepared to revise your timetable before you bury your dream! Every passing hour of every passing day and every new month increase the possibility that things will turn around. What you may need is not more faith, but more patience. The impossible may become possible when you take the long look. As we walk the walk of faith, we must become more God-like. And one quality about God is his immeasurable long-suffering and patient attitude. What great impossible deeds could you accomplish if you had a forty-year goal? If you are tempted to abandon your dream—don't! (emphasis added)[6]

I've found that typically I'll reach about one-third of my goals annually, another third will see some progress, while the final third seem to die shortly after they are set. I try never to discard the latter but reevaluate them annually and carry some over to the next year.

This book took longer to write and publish than I anticipated. My doctoral studies took a year or two longer than I expected. But I was further along even with the delays than if I had waited for everything to be perfect before I started.

Before closing this section, there are two other important aspects of goal-setting that you need to remember. The first is to share your goals with someone you trust. Job 22:28 (NAS) says, "You will also decree a thing and it will be established for you; and light will shine on your ways." Then Malachi 3:16 (NAS) states, "Then those who feared the Lord spoke to one another, and the Lord listened and heard it, and a book of remembrance was written before Him for those who fear the Lord and who esteem His name."

Those two passages attest to the fact that, when you declare your goals, an unseen spiritual dynamic and energy described earlier in this chapter are released. Your commitment to a course of action is sealed when you tell someone, because now they will be free to ask you, "How are you doing with that goal?"

The second and last aspect is to have courage and act! Courage is not the absence of fear, but acting in the midst of it. David said to his son, Solomon,

> "Be strong and courageous, and do the work. Do not be afraid or discouraged, for the Lord God, my God, is with you. He will not fail you or forsake you until all the work for the service of the temple of the Lord is finished" (1 Chronicles 28:20).

Let's close by looking at one last verse from the book of Nehemiah, the story of the man who marshalled the people toward a common goal. Nehemiah 6:15 states,

> So the wall was completed on the twenty-fifth of Elul, in fifty-two days. When all our enemies heard about this, all the surrounding nations were afraid and lost their self-confidence, because they realized that this work had been done with the help of our God.

Commit to do something great for the Lord, see it through to the end, do it with creative excellence, and then watch God's enemies be disheartened. Now that you have begun to set goals, the next section will help you manage your time so that your goals can find a place in your already busy schedule.

GOLD MINE PRINCIPLE #4

TIME
MANAGEMENT

Don't Settle for Fool's Gold

*"Lazy hands make for poverty,
but diligent hands bring wealth."*—Proverbs 10:4

Chapter 17

What a Timeless Book Says About Time

An issue of *Bits and Pieces* magazine contained this thought-provoking quote from Susan Ertz: "Millions long for immortality who do not know what to do with themselves on a rainy Sunday afternoon."[1] This quote perfectly describes some people I know. They mean well and have a lot of vision, but they waste time and never seem to live up to their full potential. What's more, God's purpose suffers with them as they waste the most precious commodity of all—their time.

A while back, I came across an issue of *Christian History* magazine that focused entirely on the life and ministry of Charles Haddon Spurgeon, the great 19th century British preacher and author. Two pages were devoted to unusual facts about this productive man and his ministry, some of which pertain directly to our study of time management. Consider these facts about Spurgeon:

>•*The New Park Street Pulpit* and *The Metropolitan Tabernacle Pulpit*—the collected sermons of Spurgeon during his ministry with that congregation—fill 63 volumes. The sermons' 20-25 million words are equivalent to the 27 volumes of the ninth

edition of the Encyclopedia Britannica. The series stands as the largest set of books by a single author in the history of Christianity.

•Spurgeon typically read six books per week and could remember what he had read—and where—even years later.

•During his lifetime, Spurgeon is estimated to have preached to 10,000,000 people.

•Spurgeon spent 20 years studying the book of Psalms and writing his commentary on them, *The Treasury of David.*

•By accepting some of his many invitations to speak, Spurgeon often preached 10 times in a week.

•Spurgeon often worked 18 hours a day. Famous explorer and missionary David Livingstone once asked him, "How do you manage to do two men's work in a single day?" Spurgeon replied, "You have forgotten that there are two of us."[2]

Spurgeon was a gifted man and minister, yet he also knew how to manage his time and get the most out of every day. Who wouldn't want to leave the legacy that he did, but who is willing to pay the price that he paid?

I have subtitled this section "Don't Settle for Fool's Gold" because I've done quite a bit of reading about the California gold rush of the 1850s. During that time, people from all over the world sold all their possessions and travelled to California, often with only the clothes on their back, to search for personal fortune. Some found it, and others gave their lives in a futile search.

Imagine someone paying the price to come to California and then one day discovering a shiny object in the ground. Assuming it to be gold, they staked their claim only to find that they sold all they had not for gold, but for something that only looked like it— fool's gold.

That's how it can be with you. You can be busy and fill

each day with well-intentioned activity. You can work hard and collapse in exhaustion each night. At the end of the day, however, you may only have fool's gold to show for your work because you wasted your time working on activities that did not represent the best use of your time. They were not related to your purpose and creative gifts, and your goals were achieved, but it was fool's gold.

The writer of Ecclesiastes put it this way: "If the ax is dull and its edge unsharpened, more strength is needed but skill will bring success" (Ecclesiastes 10:10). Poor time management is like chopping wood with a dull ax; eventually you can get the job done, but it takes a lot more energy than it does if you use a sharp ax. Becoming skillful at using the resource of time helps you find the real gold you are after, and that gold is creatively functioning in your purpose while working on your goals as we discussed in the previous sections. Before we discuss how to sharpen your ax, let's take a quick look at some of what the Bible teaches about time.

1. Joshua 10:9-14

After an all-night march from Gilgal, Joshua took them by suprise. The Lord threw them into confusion before Israel, who defeated them in a great victory at Gibeon. Israel pursued them along the road going up to Beth Horon and cut them down all the way to Azekah and Makkedah. As they fled before Israel on the road down from Beth Horon to Azekah, the Lord hurled large hailstones down on them from the sky, and more of them died from the hailstones than were killed by the swords of the Israelites. On the day the Lord gave the Amorites over to Israel, Joshua said to the Lord in the presence of Israel:

'O sun, stand still over Gibeon,

O moon, over the Valley of Aijalon,'

So the sun stood still and the moon stopped, till the nation avenged itself on its enemies, as it is written in the Book of Jashar. The sun stopped in the middle of the sky and delayed going down about a full day. There has never been a day like it before or since, a day when the Lord listened to a man. Surely the Lord was fighting for Israel!

In this story, we see that Joshua needed more time to do the task that was before him. He and his army marched all night without sleep, yet the Lord strengthened the people to fight the next day. Then, when Joshua couldn't finish the battle, he prayed for the sun to stand still, and it did that very thing, and did it for a full day. So Joshua and his men stayed up for a second consecutive night to finish the job. I know how tired I can be after only a few hours of sleep, but Joshua and his men were up for 72 hours and could still function!

Some commentators interpret the sun standing still to mean that the Lord actually "froze" the sun in the same position for almost a day. Others believe that somehow the Lord empowered the people to fight, and they were able to accomplish much in an unusually short period of time; for them, it means that the sun only *seemed* to stand still.

Whatever happened, Joshua trusted the Lord for more time, and he got it. Because Joshua knew what the real gold was, he efficiently used the time he had and then exercised faith for the extra time he needed to do the job. He refused to settle for fool's gold.

I'm sure that you're learning to trust the Lord for finances, necessary changes in your heart, and ministry or career opportunities. But you must also learn to trust Him for time, for He is Lord even over your time. He can do miraculous things for you just as He did for Joshua.

2. Ecclesiastes 3:1-8

There is a time for everything,
and a season for every activity under heaven: a time

135

to be born and a time to die,

a time to plant and a time to uproot, a time to kill and a time to heal,

a time to tear down and a time to build, a time to weep and a time to laugh,

a time to mourn and a time to dance,

a time to scatter stones and a time to gather them, a time to embrace and a time to refrain,

a time to search and a time to give up,

a time to keep and a time to throw away, a time to tear and a time to mend,

a time to be silent and a time to speak, a time to love and a time to hate,

a time for war and a time for peace.

There once was a time when I read that passage and wondered, "How can I know for sure what time and season it is? How can I know when to tear down or build? Speak or be silent? Search or give up searching?"

Gold Nugget #15

"He who gathers crops in summer is a wise son, but he who sleeps during harvest is a disgraceful son."
—Proverbs 10:5

The answers to those questions couldn't be found in a system with rules of what to do and how to do it in every situation. There were simply too many options before me every day to try and follow a set of rules. I began to find my answers to those questions first in 1 Chronicles 12:32, which describes the men of Issachar as those "who understood the times and knew what Israel should do."

The sons of Issachar, like Joshua before them, knew what they should do. They knew that it was the season to install David as king, and they gave their time to accomplish that task. If they knew where to invest their time, I determined that I could, too.

Yet how did they know for sure?

That led me to John 7:17, which states, "If anyone chooses to do God's will, he will find out." That told me if I would commit to do God's will in every situation *before* I knew what it was, He would show me what His will was for my life and my time. Finally, I read that "those who are led by the Spirit of God are sons of God" (Romans 8:14), and my answer was complete. Since I was a son of God, His Spirit would lead me to know what time it is if I am committed to do God's will, whatever it is.

After all, if God wants me to do His will—and He does—then He must reveal to me (and you) what His will is. If I open the lines of communication by surrendering my veto power over what God says before I know what He will say, then the great Communicator will reveal His will. Note also that this commitment to do before I know is an expression of faith, our next and last Gold Mine Principle.

For me, that's the basic secret to good time management. The Spirit is able to help you sort out your priorities and lead you in the way you should spend your time, if you really want to know. There can never be one set of rules to govern every situation that will come your way; on one day it will be time to build, and on the next it will be time to tear down. Only the Spirit can show you what needs to be done, and then only you can decide to spend your time on what the Spirit directs you to do.

3. Proverbs 3:1-2

"Keep my commands in your heart, for they will prolong your life many years."

Some time management systems and advisors try to help you squeeze more time from every day, and some even promise to help you find two hours or more per day. But better organization isn't the way to get more time. Obedience to God's will is the only way you can really get more time.

If you obey what the Spirit directs you to do, your obedience will extend your years and expand the amount of time you have available. That's what happened to Joshua, and it will happen to you. There are many times when I have had a lot to do. Yet when I have followed the Lord's will for my time, He has supernaturally given me more time to catch up with things. There were times when I spent time with my children even though I had a report to work on. There were other times when I gave up what I was working on to obey my supervisor's request for an urgent item. There were times when I prayed even though I had an early meeting for which I hadn't prepared. In each case, the Lord helped me with the time I had left because I trusted Him by obeying His will for the time I had. He truly can prolong the days of your life if you keep His commands in your heart.

Gold Nugget #16

"For through me your days will be many, and years will be added to your life."
—Proverbs 9:11

4. 2 Peter 3:8

Another important aspect of time for you to understand is that God is seldom in a hurry, nor is He ever late. The Lord isn't committed to our concept of time, but expects us to walk according to His perspective. Peter gave us some important insight when he wrote, "But do not forget this one thing, dear friends: With the Lord a day is like a thousand years, and a thousand years are like a day." I always thought that sounded so spiritual until one day I did some simple math and came up with a better understanding.

If you divide 24 hours into 1,000 years, you can see that each hour with the Lord is the equivalent of almost 42 years; if you divide 60 minutes into 42 years, each minute is like 8.5 months; if you divide 60 seconds into 8.5 months, you see that every second to the Lord is like four days! So if the Lord tells you He'll be there in a minute, you may have to wait more than eight months, or just a second may take four days.

Isaiah wrote, "Those who wait for the Lord will gain new strength" (Isaiah 40:31 NAS). My time management can never circumvent the fact that the Lord is in control. I can't make anything happen unless it's in His time; the harder I try, the more frustrated I can become. There are some things that just have to wait, and I can't do anything about it.

At the same time, the verse in 2 Peter says that 1,000 years is like a day. That means if I think something may require nine months to complete, I may be able to complete it in just a minute. Often, I don't engage a project because I don't believe I have enough time, and I am *afraid* (there is the fear factor) I won't be able to do it well. This verse indicates that if I have faith for time, God can do the unexpected and help me accomplish more than I thought possible. That is how I have written my books, and even as I edit this book, I am trusting God for the time it will take—time which I did not think I had.

5. Ephesians 5:15-16

This verse is worth looking at in several different translations. It says,

"Be careful then how you live...making the very most of the time" (AMP).

...make the most of every opportunity to do good" (LB).

...making the most of your time" (NAS).

...make the best possible use of your time" (Phillips).

Paul urged the Ephesians to make the most of their time, and that exhortation applies to you today. There's only one way to make the most of your time, and that's to spend it on activities that will bring the greatest return for the Lord and His kingdom. Don't take a trip and just stare out the window for hours; don't spend a good part of your day in front of the television set. Don't settle for fool's gold, but use your time to go after the most important issues—the real gold—that are worthy of your efforts. The real gold is found in your purpose, as you set goals that release your creativity to achieve what is most important to you.

Covey refers to the real gold in life as "Quadrant II"

activities—activities that are not urgent but important.

> Quadrant II is the heart of effective personal management.... It deals with things like building relationships, writing a personal mission statement, long-range planning, exercising, preventive maintenance, preparation— all those things we know we need to do, but somehow seldom get around to doing, because they aren't urgent. To paraphrase Peter Drucker, effective people are not problem-minded; they're opportunity-minded. They feed opportunities and starve problems. They think preventively.[3]

The Lord expects you not to be not a victim of time that slipped away, but one who redeems the time. If you could free up 15 minutes every day for one year to read the Bible, for example, at the end of the year you would have read the equivalent of 3.8 full days! Begin to seize those moments that you have wasted away. Over a period of time they will add up.

I began writing a Bible devotional commentary in 2001. I promised that I would send out to my subscribers a seven-day devotional every week that focused on four New Testament verses per day. I kept that up day after day, week after week, year after year. In 2009, I had covered every verse in the New Testament! What could you do if you had that kind of daily focus, and did a little at a time over a long period of time? At this moment, I am publishing those devotionals that will create a 12-volume *Live the Word* commentary series that will be around until the Lord returns, probably long after I am gone.

6. Proverbs 18:9

Before we close, there's just one more point to make. If you don't do something that needs to be done, you have acted just like someone who took what was done and undid it! Proverbs 18:9 states, "One who is slack in his work is brother to one who destroys." Your inability to do the important things is the same thing as getting them done and then tearing them apart. If you build a shed and then burn it down or don't build the shed in the first place, isn't the end result the same?

If you miss an opportunity that God has given you, you're related to one who would destroy. You may think, "It's no big deal; nobody got hurt because I didn't learn Spanish," or "Nobody suffered because I didn't start that business." That may be true, but you don't really know what would have happened had you started and completed those goals.

If you feel I am putting you under some pressure to produce as you read that statement, that's good. Paul urged the Corinthians "not to receive God's grace in vain" (2 Corinthians 6:1). If he warned not to do that, then it must be possible to receive God's grace in such a way that the Lord gets no return on His investment. God's grace has come to your life, but He has work for you to do. So roll up your sleeves and let's look at some principles that will help you achieve efficiency through better time management.

Chapter 18

How to Be
a Wise Guy (or Gal)

When you think of it, time is the great equalizer. You may not have as much talent or money as others, but you have as many hours in the day as they do, as many as Bill Gates, or Martin Luther King, Jr., or John Maxwell, or Mahatma Gandhi. You have the same opportunity as they had to maximize your efforts so that, at the end of the day, you can know you did the things the Lord put before you to do, the things that were in your heart to do.

In the first edition of this book, I titled this section efficiency. I have changed the wording, but efficiency is still at the heart of what I want you to obtain as you apply this fourth Gold Mine Principle of time. Before we go on, let's define the term "efficiency" to mean *the ability to get supernatural results using limited human, financial, and physical resources.* Joshua was an efficient general who used his limited time and fighting men to win the battle. Gideon routed the Midianites not with the 32,000 men with which he started, but with the 200 men who survived the tests of bravery and watchfulness.

Jesus took five loaves and two fish and fed 5,000 people with plenty of leftovers. Paul, in a matter of a few decades, had planted enough regional churches to reach most of the known world. In each case, those men worked efficiently because they used their time well, and God empowered the time they had to efficiently produce supernatural results. No one stressed or had a heart attack trying to do more than was humanly possible. They did go beyond human limitations, but it was because God empowered them to do so, just like He did Charles Spurgeon—or John Stanko.

A popular saying goes, "If you want something done, ask a busy person to do it." It seems as if those who manage their time well can almost always fit something else in. When someone approaches me about a job or a request for help, I try to find how I can do it instead of how I can't. While I was editing this section, someone from England wrote me on Facebook to talk about how she can be in a different place next year at this time. We had a good conversation, and I was perfectly comfortable interrupting my editing for her needs. Then I prayed and God helped me pick up my stream of thought to continue with this work. In addition to the verses discussed in the previous chapter, I've studied three other biblical principles that have helped me tremendously in my quest for efficiency and good time management. They are wisdom, stewardship, and dominion.

Wisdom

Let's begin by defining wisdom as *the ability to use knowledge in a supernatural manner.* You need wisdom on a daily basis if you are going to manage your time well. Just having the knowledge of what to do is no guarantee that you have the know-how to apply that knowledge; that comes only through wisdom.

Every day you're faced with so many things you can do and need to do. But you're also faced with many interruptions—just like I was last evening—and you have limited time resources. On top of all that, you have the human pressures that come against you such as depression, fatigue, doubt, and fear. These things try to keep you from being productive and becoming all that God wants you to be. Given those realities, you need wisdom. To move from knowing what to do to actually doing it requires wisdom.

Wisdom isn't some sage sitting cross-legged with his disciples gathered around him as he pontificates, nor is it a system of beliefs, new ideas, or philosophies as the ancient Greeks supposed. Wisdom for you and me is a person—our Lord Jesus Christ. Paul wrote to the Colossians about this Christ, "in whom are hidden all the treasures of wisdom and knowledge" (Colossians 2:3) and to the Corinthians about Christ, "the power of God and the wisdom of God" (1 Corinthians 1:24). Paul understood clearly that our wisdom was a man, not a concept.

That's why a set of rules can't possibly cover every time management scenario you will face. Carnal or religious people (as opposed to spiritual folks) craves a system because when they have a system, they no longer need to rely on the Lord. If you had a foolproof guide of how to plan every day in every way, you would carry on in your own understanding without any need for the Lord's input. You have need of wisdom and that comes from a vibrant, meaningful relationship with a living God who is able to communicate clearly to you in every situation. Your efficiency will come from a living word from a living God that will energize you to do more with less because He is strengthening you to do it.

It's interesting what Solomon asked for when he became king. He didn't actually ask for wisdom to rule, but for a "discerning [understanding] heart" (1 Kings 3:9). He wanted to be able to hear what the Lord was directing him to do. Because he didn't ask for money or the death of his enemies, the Lord granted his prayer.

> God gave Solomon wisdom and very great insight, and a breadth of understanding as measureless as the sand on the seashore. Solomon's wisdom was greater than the wisdom of all the men of the East, and greater than all the wisdom of Egypt. He was wiser than any other man.... And his fame spread to all the surrounding nations. He spoke three thousand proverbs and his songs numbered a thousand and five. He described plant life, from

the cedar of Lebanon to the hyssop that grows out of walls. He also taught about animals and birds, reptiles and fish. Men of all nations came to listen to Solomon's wisdom, sent by all the kings of the world, who had heard of his wisdom (1 Kings 4:29-34).

You might say that Solomon was efficient, writing songs, poems, riddles, and exploring the glories of God's creation. He took his limited resources and added them to God's limitless resources. The results were awesome and a wonderful example of synergy, which we discussed earlier!

You need that same listening heart. One problem you will encounter as you listen, however, is that there are many voices vying for your attention. Proverbs 9 depicts both Wisdom and Folly sitting on the high places of the city and "calling out to those who pass by" (Proverbs 9:15). When you pray, do you suddenly think of all kinds of things you have to do? When you prepare to work at your desk, in your shop, or at the kitchen counter, do projects other than the one before you cry out for your attention? Because Solomon realized his propensity to be overwhelmed by these urgent voices to do so many things, he asked for a listening heart so he could manage his time and life well.

You should also ask for wisdom to know how to use your time and energies. And when you do, the Lord will say to you what He said to Solomon:

> "Since you have asked for this and not for long life or wealth for yourself, nor have asked for the death of your enemies but for discernment in administering justice, I will do what you have asked. I will give you a wise and discerning heart" (1 Kings 3:11-12).

So wisdom is neither a set of beliefs nor is it a teaching. Godly wisdom is best expressed by someone creatively doing new things in new ways. A system requires that you follow what someone else has developed for their world. That system may not fit into your world, however, because the Lord has put something before you to do that's unique. I want to face new challenges and find new solutions, perhaps combining old techniques in some new manner in a way that is consistent with who I am. I want to do things that haven't been done and not merely replicate what's already been done.

Proverbs 8 captures the essence of this creative wisdom, and we looked at this passage when we discussed the second Gold Mine Principle of creativity:

> The Lord brought me forth as the first of his works, before his deeds of old; I was appointed from eternity, from the beginning, before the world began. When there were no oceans, I was given birth, when there were no springs abounding with water; before the mountains were settled in place, before the hills, I was given birth, before he made the earth or his fields or any of the dust of the world. I was there when he set the heavens in place, when he marked out the horizon on the face of the deep, when he established the clouds above and fixed securely the fountains of the deep, when he gave the sea its boundary so the waters would not overstep his command, and when he marked out the foundations of the earth. Then I was the craftsman at his side. I was filled with delight day after day, rejoicing always in his presence, rejoicing in his whole world and delighting in mankind (verses 22-31).

The Lord used wisdom to create the world. There was no book He could refer to in order to do it right the first time. Proverbs 8 tells us that wisdom was His guide, the same wisdom that's available to you. If every day in your life presents new situations you've never faced before, then only wisdom will help you work them out. And since you know that wisdom is a person, then you know that Proverbs 8 is actually Jesus speaking. The wisdom that leads to efficiency involves learning how to listen and then having the confidence that you can apply what you've heard to a new and unique situation.

Wisdom that leads to a creative solution or efficient use of resources always produces awe for the sovereignty and power of God. Solomon's first test after he asked for wisdom was the case of the two women and the baby. One woman claimed the baby was hers, and the other claimed she was lying. What was Solomon to do? He couldn't ask his father, nor did he have a law library close at hand. So he told them to cut the baby in half with a sword and give half to each woman. The real mother said to give the baby to the other woman. Based on her response, Solomon awarded her the baby. Where did he get that idea from? Solomon was listening, and it resulted in true justice for the real mother. "When all Israel heard the verdict the king had given, they held the king in awe, because they saw that he had wisdom from God to administer justice" (1 Kings 3:28). I want people to hold the Lord in awe because I have wisdom to efficiently run my world and responsibilities.

> ### Gold Nugget #17
> "By wisdom the Lord laid the earth's foundations, by understanding he set the heavens in place."
> —Proverbs 3:19

There are four ways that you can get this divine wisdom. First, you seek it like Solomon did. Proverbs 2:4-6 says,

> If you look for it [wisdom] as for silver and search for it [wisdom] as for hidden treasure, then you will understand the fear of the Lord and find the knowledge of God. For the Lord gives wisdom; and from his mouth come knowledge and understanding.

Imagine that someone gave you a guarantee that there was a gold bar buried in your backyard. Would you stop searching for it just because you didn't find it after you dug one hole? You would probably dig up your entire yard until you did find it.

That's the kind of urgency and diligence you must apply if you're going to find godly wisdom. You have a guarantee that it's there, but you must seek it. When Nebuchadnezzar gave the order for all the wise men in Babylon to be killed, Daniel sought the Lord for wisdom and received the interpretation to an unknown dream. He got the wisdom he needed because he desperately sought it, and his life depended on finding it.

During a transition in my life, I fasted 21 days because I needed the wisdom of God. I was desperate to find the wisdom and understanding that the Lord has promised. You don't find God's wisdom by praying "now-I-lay-me-down-to-sleep" prayers. You find it by paying a price, the same price that even Jesus had to pay. The writer of Hebrews painted a striking picture of Jesus' prayer life when he wrote,

> During the days of Jesus' life on earth, he offered up prayers and petitions with loud cries and tears to the one who could save him from death, and he was heard because of his reverent submission. Although he was a son, he learned obedience from what he suffered and, once made perfect, he became the source of eternal salvation for all who obey him (Hebrews 5:7-10).

Jesus prayed with a loud voice and tearful cries. He didn't use King James' English and address His Father with a religious "Thee" and "Thou." He cried out and received what He asked for. If that's the pattern that Jesus used, will you be heard with any less effort or commitment? Jesus was heard not because He was God; He was heard because He paid the price to be heard.

After you seek wisdom, the next step is to learn to listen to the Spirit who is speaking. As Jesus was about to choose His 12 apostles, Luke wrote,

> One of those days Jesus went out to a mountainside to pray, and *spent the night praying to God.* When morning came, he called his disciples to him and chose twelve of them, whom he also designated apostles (Luke 6:12-13, emphasis added).

Jesus lost a night's sleep praying and listening; afterward, He chose 12 men to be "apostles," something that had no religious precedent. He did something new with God's wisdom and dug deep to find it. Those 12 men, representing a new way of doing things, turned the world upside down. Godly wisdom will help turn your world upside down as well, if you learn to listen and discern what the Lord is saying.

Now you may be concerned about how you will know if the Lord is speaking to you. The only guarantee is found in Hebrews 11:6, where you're told, "Without faith it is impossible to please God, because anyone who comes to him must believe that he exists and that he rewards those who earnestly seek him." If you diligently seek Him, He will make Himself known somehow. It may be through someone else, circumstances, or a small still voice, but He will make Himself known and heard. Your faith will always be rewarded. God is a great communicator and you should put your faith in His ability to speak, not your ability to hear.

The first step to get wisdom is seeking and the second step is listening. The third step is to study the book of Proverbs. Early in my Christian walk, someone told me to read one chapter from Proverbs every day. Since there were 31 chapters and most months have 31 days, it would therefore be possible to finish the entire book in one month. I did this faithfully, but found I wasn't gaining much ground in retaining what the book had to say.

It seemed that most chapters jumped from topic to topic with no common theme. A typical chapter would talk about righteousness, speech, finances, leadership, family, and fools. One day I realized that the book was written that way on purpose so the casual reader would not get much out of it. If I was going to understand Proverbs, I knew I would have to do a lot more work than just read it once a day.

So I started to identify seven major themes of Proverbs and placed each verse in the category where it belonged. When I got my first computer, I categorized each verse so that at any time I could reference what Proverbs had to say about money or leadership quickly and efficiently. As a pastor, I began to do most of my marital counseling out of the book of Proverbs.

I took the time to study that book and haven't stopped. I've tried to dig out the nuggets of gold contained in every chapter and make them part of my life and behavior. While all Scripture gives wisdom, none but Proverbs was written with that express purpose:

> *For attaining wisdom* and discipline; for under-standing words of insight; for acquiring a disciplined and prudent life, doing what is right and just and fair; for giving prudence to the simple, knowledge and discretion to the young—*let the wise listen and add to their learning,* and let the discerning get guidance (Proverbs 1:2-5, emphasis added).

If you need wisdom in your life, then you need the book of Proverbs more than ever before. It was written with the goal of giving you wisdom, but it won't come easily. You will have to dig, study, and read. For those who pay the price, however, Proverbs holds priceless gems of wisdom that can make the dif-ference between success and failure.

The fourth and final way to get wisdom is to walk with the wise. "He who walks with the wise grows wise, but a com-panion of fools suffers harm" (Proverbs 13:20). I've tried to make it a habit of finding wise men and women of God and walking as close to them as possible. My marriage and children are better for it, and my business is as well. I have actually written about what I call having a personal board of directors. This is a board that serves you to mentor and train you for the purpose and creativity God has assigned you. These members may be living or gone, and if they are gone, their writings, biographies, and tes-timonies can still lead and guide you, serving to direct your work and personal development. Who would serve on your personal board of directors?

The "me-and-Jesus" mentality so prevalent in the modern believer wasn't the mentality in the early Church. They ministered and functioned in teams and learned to draw on one another's strengths. Learning only from your own expe-rience isn't the best teacher. Learning from others' experiences, especially their mistakes, is a better and more efficient way. And you can do that by following them closely.

If you're disorganized or don't manage your time well, the best thing you can do is find people who are organized and spend time with them. Let them give you some balance and another perspective of how to do things. If you can't walk with the wise, you can at least read their literature. My goal is to read two books every month—one with theological content and one with management or leadership principles. And I try to read authors who have been successful in their field, not those who have an idea that should work but remains untested. Remember, wisdom isn't just ideas, but someone creatively applying knowledge that God gives to do new things. I want to learn from those who have experience so that I can be equipped to do what is now before me. If you know you need more wisdom than you have now, pray this prayer:

> Lord, I need wisdom. I don't use my time as well as I could or should. I need Your wisdom so I can be more efficient. From now on, I will ask You for more wisdom and then listen and watch for Your reply; I will more diligently study the book of Proverbs and I will make every effort to walk with the wise, through relationships, books, conferences, or other media. Help me, Lord. Your word says, "If any of you lacks wisdom, he should ask God who gives generously to all without finding fault, and it will be given to him. But when he asks, he must believe and not doubt" (James 1:5-6). I'm asking You now, believing that You will give me the wisdom I need according to Your promise. Thank You for hearing me, Lord. Amen.

And now that you're on your way toward getting wisdom, let's study the next concept that will lead to a more efficient life.

Chapter 19

The Practical

Even with the wisdom of God and God's help, time management is one of the toughest disciplines in life, but critical to achieving purpose and goals. Truth be told, we *all* need help where time management is concerned. The problem is that time management is not really what we should be discussing.

Time management is the wrong definition of what you need. You don't need help managing time, for time cannot be managed. It goes by at the same pace it always has. You cannot save it, slow it down, speed it up, or recover it once it's gone. *You cannot manage time; you can only manage the events that occur within the time that you have.* Rather than call it time management, perhaps we should really think of it as event management.

Let me give you an example. There is nothing special about 6 AM, until you set your alarm for 6 AM. The wakeup call is the event that takes place at 6 AM. Then you have to be at work at 7:30, so you must manage a series of events to ensure you are there on time. Those events include showering, breakfast, devotions, getting the children off, and the commute to work. There is nothing you can do about the 90 minutes to get to work from the time you get out of bed; it will pass as every 90-minute segment of time has always passed. There are a lot of things you can do, however, to manage the events that occur in those 90 minutes. What you do in them will determine whether or not you are successful, defined by being on time or late for work.

The rest of your life is like that as well. You have 24

hours every day; you just don't know how many 24 hour units you have ahead of you. My mother passed away at 92 years of age; a young child of five who attended my church was killed in a house fire a few years ago. Your times are truly in His hands, and you have the duty and joy of making the most of every day that you have on earth. You will do that by managing the events therein as best you can.

When you think of it, you have all the time in the world. You have 24 hours for every day you are alive, the same as everyone else. Then why can some produce so much and others seem to struggle just to get through the day? It's because the productive person understands the difference between time and event control.

Peter Drucker, when discussing the issue of leadership focus, tells an interesting story about the composer Mozart:

> Very few people know where they belong, what kind of temperament and person they are. "Do I work with people, or am I a loner?" And "What are my values? What am I committed to?" And "Where do I belong? What is my contribution?"
>
> And this is, as I said, unprecedented. Those questions were never asked—well, yes, the super achievers asked them. Leonardo DaVinci had one whole notebook in which he asked these questions of himself. And Mozart knew it and knew it very well. He's the only man in the history of music who was equally good on two totally different instruments. He wasn't only a great piano virtuoso; he was an incredible violin virtuoso. And yet, he decided you can only be good in one instrument, because to be good, you have to practice three hours a day. There are not enough hours a day, and so he gave up the violin. He knew it, and he wrote it down. We have his notebooks.
>
> The super achievers always knew when to say "No." And they always knew what to reach for. And

they always knew where to place themselves. That makes them super achievers. And now all of us will have to learn that. It's not very difficult. The key to it is—what Leonardo did and Mozart did—is to write it down and then check it.[4]

Can you imagine being equally world-class in two things and quitting one of them? That really is unprecedented. Mozart, however, still impacts the world with his music because he realized that he had all the time in the world—but not all the time he needed. He realized that he was finite and had to make choices about what to do with his time, with those 24 hours a day available to each and every leader. With that in mind, he quit one instrument to concentrate on the other. Notice that Drucker spoke of values, knowing what's important to you. Those values should guide your decisions on what to do and what not to do. It helps when you write your values out and check your progress and focus from time to time (we will discuss developing your values in the next chapter).

When I talk of time management in a seminar setting, I usually share my six time-management friends—principles and skills that have made me more effective in the management of my time. In the original version of this book, there were only four, but I have added two more over the last twenty years, and here they are for your consideration:

1. The book of Proverbs

By now, I guess you know that I love the book of Proverbs in the Old Testament. I've studied it for 35 years and I still find things I'd never seen before. What I like best is how practical it is. It contains much useful information on how to live life and how to lead. To my surprise, it also contains material on how to manage time.

To effectively manage your time, you need wisdom as we discussed in the last chapter. Wisdom enables you to creatively do things that you've never done before. That's important in time management because every day is different and presents new opportunities and challenges. As you enter new seasons of your life, you need wisdom as well to navigate the challenges of staying on course and focused.

The daily readings in my books, *A Daily Dose of Proverbs* and *A Daily Taste of Proverbs*, contain many insights on effective time management, and I encourage you to use them as a daily guide to help you prioritize your world. For the sake of this discussion, let me quote only one verse that has become my "friend" as I manage my time: "For by me [wisdom] your days will be multiplied, and years of life will be added to you" (Proverbs 9:11 NAS).

From that verse, I see that I can effectively "multiply" my days and consequently my effectiveness by applying wisdom where time is concerned. Since Proverbs is a source of wisdom, it's my first friend where time management is concerned.

2. A time management system

I formerly used the classic size, Monticello-style Franklin Covey time management system as my notebook to write things down as Drucker recommended. It had two pages for every day of the year and it gave me room to include my prioritized daily task list (something I do almost every day), notes from daily meetings, meeting agendas, and discussion lists for each of my key staff people that include what they are working on. Today, I don't use that system any longer.

I used to teach that a yellow tablet and spiral notebook aren't systems. They are places to write things down, but there's little or no chance of retrieving what you record in one of them. With so much technology available now, however, I have changed my thinking, and I now use a zippered, tablet-sized notebook that carries a yellow tablet. I then use index cards to make my daily to-do lists, which I still prioritize and carry with me everywhere I go. When someone sees me write something to do in my notebook, they still know it's as good as done because I'm committed to use that simple system to keep me focused and on task.

The key is not which system you use, but how you use it. I have a friend who is an organizational consultant, and her advice to clients (and to me) is that we should not go through work to get to work. My notebook, as simple as it is, is easy to use, and I have a system that helps me find things easily. I don't throw away any list until I have accomplished everything on it, or until I have transferred those things not done to a new list. If you would see me in a coffee shop with some time on my hands, you would see me going through my lists and cards to create new master lists and then a daily list to focus my efforts. When I am in the car, I am listening to an audio book or making phone calls to people on my list to call.

The point is to take all your thoughts and ideas seriously by writing them down. Then review those ideas to see what should make it to your daily to-do list. If your day is busy and most of your time is beyond your control at work or with family, then all the more reason to have a list. If you have just a small amount of discretionary time and you don't have something to keep your priorities in front of you, you will waste that time, and it may add up to large amounts of time wasted in small amounts.

3. My tech toys

Since the first edition of *Life is a Gold Mine*, there are a host of high tech resources to be used to help with time management. I have an iPhone and I use it for my calendar, email, and some to-do lists. My phone is always with me, even when my notebook is not, but I still like the feel of pen on the paper to plan my days. I will use the smartphone for certain things, but I stopped using my laptop computer for much that is related to time management. I need something that is always with me, and the smartphone qualifies.

4. When in doubt, throw it out!

A time management expert advised me one time not to go through work to get to work. I listened to what she told me and I am ruthless when it comes to paperwork. At least twice a year, I "clean out" my office and home files, books, and articles. I refuse to keep anything that I can easily retrieve through some other source. I do the same thing with my computer and regularly work to dump files that I haven't used in the previous 12 months.

I don't like to look at stacks of "stuff" that accumulate because I may need them one day. I especially don't like wading through piles to find what I need. So I have an adequate filing system and throw out lots of papers and letters. If there's any doubt, then I usually throw it out and have seldom had any regrets. This philosophy has saved me a lot of time and trouble, and kept my busy world streamlined and efficient.

5. Delegation

I've found that if I build a team, I have more people around me who may enjoy doing something that I dread or tolerate. Delegation also rewards people for hard work by giving them more responsibility and challenge in the workplace.

Alec MacKenzie, time management author and expert, wrote, "The two key points to keep in mind about delegation: Do it (so you don't spend time doing things others could or should be doing) and do it right (so you won't have to spend time undoing a poor job)."[5] Delegation isn't abandoning tasks and people but rather working with the team to help them be successful and to grow in their abilities and responsibilities. Delegation is my time management friend because it allows me to expand my leadership without dominating the followers.

6. Written goals

We discussed written goals in Section Three, but it bears repeating in this section. I like to write out my goals for the coming year and have done so for a number of years. Merrill and Donna Douglass said it best when they wrote:

> Many of us think that writing goals is unnecessary. We often say that we keep goals in our head, and as long as we think about them it doesn't matter

whether or not the goals are written down. This is dangerous reasoning. The purpose of writing goals is to clarify them. There seems to be a special kind of magic in writing goals. Once a goal is written, you have more invested in it than before.[6]

My goals come from my values and tell me what is important. My goals keep me (most of the time) from investing time in matters that aren't important. For instance, I originally wanted to write a book every year for the next ten years. That goal kept me focused when I traveled and when I was home, as other things were clamoring for my attention and time. Now my goal is write as many books as possible in a year, and this past year, I published six, although some were of material I had written in past years. My point is that my written goals keep me on task and on target, and they help me say no to some things that may sap my time.

So let's review. The six friends that keep me from wasting all the time in my world are:

- The book of Proverbs
- A time management system
- My tech toys
- When in doubt, throw it out!
- Delegation
- Written goals

How many of these items or concepts are in your life? Are there other things that aren't included that have helped you use your time more effectively? I hope there are, because my desire would be for you to manage your time well to express your purpose and creativity. Let's move on now to look at some more practical tips to manage your daily to-do list.

Chapter 20
Your Values

In the first edition of this book, I included a discussion of stewardship and dominion, two concepts that are important where time management is concerned. First, we recognize that our time is not our own—it belongs to God and as He directs, to others. That means we do not own our calendars, but rather we act as stewards over them. When we have proved that we are faithful and can be trusted with time, then we transition to dominion, where we have more say and make more decisions where our time management is concerned. There was a day when I served others and proved that I could be a good steward over the things of another. When that season was finished, I was then promoted to situations where I could decide what my priorities were and where I would invest my time and energy.

I also included a time inventory in the first edition. I recommended that readers do an analysis of where their time was going so they could make adjustments based on reality. I used the example that I would regularly report in my seminars that I seldom watched television. Then I did a time inventory, and discovered that in one week, I had watched 14 hours of TV. So much for not watching TV that much! Granted, I watched late at night when I would not have been doing much else except sleep, but the 14 hours shocked me, and I could not deny the truth. As I edit this book, it is 8 PM on a Thursday evening, and I am investing my time in this revision as opposed to leisure time.

That decision tonight is one that is consistent with my governing values—principles that I have identified that are important to me and thus help govern or guide my decisions of how I use my time. As I've studied successful leaders, I've seen that they have almost always developed an inner set of values, whether they are aware that they have or not. Each one has a set of guidelines that help them make decisions, small or great. Some have written down these values and carry them in a notebook or planner; others carry them on the "tablets of their heart." Most often these values were developed and defined from:

- Family examples, both positive and negative
- Mentoring relationships
- Religious teachings
- Life failures
- Suffering through tough times
- Watching other leaders whom they admired
- Watching other leaders whom they did *not* admire

For instance, some who were taken advantage of have vowed never to do the same, and others, out of the same situation, decided to take advantage of as many people as possible. Both have developed values that guide their decisions and develop their leadership style. Others have felt the pain of domineering leadership and decided to perpetuate that style; some hold the value not to rule with an iron fist, but rather with an open hand. Both have developed values. And without realizing it, you have developed some values, too.

Robert Greenleaf, in his book, *On Becoming a Servant Leader*, stated "This is the ultimate test: what values govern one's life — at the end of it?" He poses an interesting question, don't you think?

Are you developing a set of values that adjust over your lifetime as your leadership grows and matures? You shouldn't wait until you're a leader to try to define these values, for by then you may not see the importance of such a task ("I'm already a leader; why sweat the small stuff now when big decisions await?"). If you wait too long to reflect on your values, you may find that you've already given your energy to values that weren't worth the effort you gave them.

As most successful leaders, the Apostle Paul had a set of values that guided his ministry and ministry decisions:

1. Not taking financial support from the churches he was starting

2. Not working where someone had already labored to start a church

3. Always visiting the synagogue first when arriving in an area

4. Traveling in the company of a team

5. Not insisting on a Jewish lifestyle as he visited diverse cultures and people

Paul's success wasn't a matter of chance. At least part of his success came from the fact that he had a set of values that served to guide his life and work decisions. He didn't impose these values on others, for they belonged to him, having been shaped by his own experience and understanding of what God wanted him to do.

I'm grateful to the Franklin Covey Company for helping me develop my values. While studying to become a certified time management facilitator through that company, their instructor directed all those being trained to write out our values. He told us there weren't a maximum or minimum number, and he encouraged us to write them in a positive style that related to the present ("I am"), and not the future ("I will"). Then he asked that we attempt to prioritize those values and from that point forward carry them with us for regular review and adjustment.

The company's objective was to allow us to see our values and allow them to better guide our decisions, decisions we would be making as leaders. In fact, they called these values our *governing* values, since they do, sometimes without realizing it, govern our life and decisions. I have to say that this has been a most rewarding experience. Now I regularly work with other leaders and potential leaders to help them develop a set of values that will guide (or are guiding) their life and leadership.

I offer my own values as an example of how they can be done, not as a model list of values to be held. I developed mine by identifying my favorite passages from the Bible. I then did what Franklin Covey asked me to do: Put some narrative explanation to each value and prioritize them.

Developing values, however, isn't a science with rigid rules and procedures; rather it's an art. At the end of my list, I'll make some further recommendations of how to develop your list of governing values. Keep in mind that mine are based on a Christian life and worldview and aren't offered with anything in mind except to give you a better understanding of my leadership style and what updated, prioritized governing values can look like.

Chapter 21

My Values

As I mentioned in the previous chapter, I present my values in this chapter to give you an idea of what a set of prioritized governing values look like. Your values do not have to be the same as mine, but they should be an accurate depiction of those activities and behaviors that are most important to you. Since they are important, they should govern your time decisions and help you know when to say yes and when to say no to the events that present themselves to you for your attention. At the end of this list, I will include some steps to take so you can develop your own set of values.

1. I do the will of God.

I prayed one time that I would be like Timothy, not fully realizing what I was praying. I saw Timothy in a whole new light as I read Philippians 2:19-23:

> I hope in the Lord Jesus to send Timothy to you soon, that I also may be cheered when I receive news about you. I have no one else like him, who takes a genuine interest in your welfare. For everyone looks out for his own interests and not those of Jesus Christ. But you know that Timothy has proved himself, because as a son with his father he has served with me in the work of the gospel. I hope, therefore, to send him as soon as I see how things go with me.

> The will of God, as I understand it, is to put other's

interests before my own and to *serve* in furthering the gospel as the Holy Spirit and my oversight so direct. That also requires a vibrant and diligent prayer and study life that finds the will of God and does it.

2. I walk in faith.

The writer of Hebrews wrote, "Without faith it is impossible to please God." I please the Lord by exercising faith concerning my purpose, family, finances, future, and relationships. The second part of that verse completes the thought when it says, "because anyone who comes to him must believe that he exists and that he rewards those who earnestly seek him" (Hebrews 11:6). God rewards me for my faith more than I deserve.

My faith has practical expression through my giving habits as I am generous with my time, knowledge, wisdom, and money.

3. I love my family.

The Lord has given me three wonderful gifts: Kathy, John, and Deborah. The Apostle Paul commanded husbands to love their wives,

> Just as Christ loved the church and gave himself for her to make her holy, cleansing her by the washing with water through the word, and to present her to himself as a radiant church, without stain or wrinkle or any other blemish, but holy and blameless. In the same way, husbands ought to love their wives as their own bodies (Ephesians 5:25-28).

I love my wife and release her to her purpose as a joint heir with me of the gracious gift of life (1 Peter 3:7). He also told fathers not to "embitter your children, or they will become discouraged" (Colossians 3:21). I am a friend and encourager to my children and help release them to their God-given purpose.

4. I am a communicator.

Jesus was a great communicator. Mark reported that "the large crowd listened to him [Jesus] with delight" (Mark 12:37). That came from His insight into the Word, His love for people, and His effective speaking style. I follow in His footsteps. Jesus also said, "The Father who sent me commanded me what to say and how to say it" (John 12:49).

I have something to say and know how to present it with clarity, humor, and conviction, whether speaking, writing books and articles, or communicating through other media. (such as the Internet, radio and video). I study and effectively utilize humor to enhance my ability to communicate with others.

5. I am a servant leader.

Because I am a man of purpose, I express my purpose by serving the world in many capacities. Since my childhood, I've also found myself in leadership positions. Thus I combine those two roles—servant and leader—to be a servant leader from a biblical perspective. I lead and serve according to God's will and implement my decisions in the right spirit and attitude. Peter wrote,

> Be shepherds of God's flock that is under your care, serving as overseers — not because you must, but because you are willing, as God wants you to be; not greedy for money, but eager to serve; not lording it over those entrusted to you, but being examples to the flock (1 Peter 5:2-3).

I lead in the tradition of Jesus, Moses, Joseph, David, Solomon, and Daniel. I grow in my understanding of servant leadership, learning to listen well and to influence, not control others. I am also a leader of integrity and courage.

6. I am a team player.

I've been an avid sports fan since my youth. I now realize that this was simply a love for the team concept that's so vital to, yet so absent from, much of management and ministry today. I help others identify their life's purpose and then train and coach them to work with other people of purpose. I pursue the synergy that comes from teamwork when everyone has a chance to communicate and share their creativity in an open atmosphere as free from authoritarian techniques as possible.

The Apostle Paul almost always traveled in a team and was released into ministry from the context of "team" in Acts 13:1-3:

> In the church at Antioch there were prophets and teachers: Barnabas, Simeon called Niger, Lucius of Cyrene, Manaen (who had been brought up with Herod the tetrarch) and Saul. While they were worshiping the Lord and fasting, the Holy Spirit said, "Set apart for me Barnabas and Saul for the work to which I have called them." So after they had fasted and prayed, they placed their hands on them and sent them off.

7. I am a reconciler.

The gospel of Jesus Christ is the only answer to society's problems and that includes racism. I work with people of color and of various cultures to model relationships that will help reconcile people to God and then to one another. As Paul wrote in 2 Corinthians 5:18-20,

> All this is from God, who reconciled us to himself through Christ and gave us the ministry of reconciliation; that God was reconciling the world to himself in Christ, not counting men's sins against them. And he has committed to us the message of reconciliation. We are therefore Christ's ambassadors, as though God were making his appeal through us. We implore you on Christ's behalf: Be reconciled to God.

I mentor young men and women to equip them to be all they can be in God and affirm their beauty and worth in God's eyes.

8. I am a learner.

Because the world is changing so rapidly, I can't afford to "crystallize" in my work habits or thinking. Paul wrote, "All Scripture is God-breathed and is useful for teaching, rebuking, correcting and training in righteousness, so that the man of God may be thoroughly equipped for every good work" (2 Timothy

3:16). That means I must continue to learn and grow in the knowledge of God (Colossians 1:10). My primary focus is the word of God and my prayer is "open my eyes that I may see wonderful things in your law" (Psalm 119:18).

I read, study, take classes, attend seminars, learn from role models, and master new techniques and technology that enable me to learn until my strength fails or I die.

9. I am energetic.

"I became a servant of this gospel by the gift of God's grace given me through the working of his power" (Ephesians 3:7). Paul accomplished his life purpose "through the working of his [God's] power." The Greek word for "working" is *energeo*. I apply this same *energeo* in my life and do not work in my own strength. I maintain this energy by staying focused on my purpose, eating healthy food, exercising, and getting appropriate rest. I use this energy to produce more than I consume and to engage in activities that brings increase and glory to God.

When I work, I work and walk in the truth of what Paul wrote to the Corinthians:

> But by the grace of God I am what I am, and His grace toward me did not prove vain; but I labored even more than all of them, yet not I, but the grace of God with me (1 Corinthians 15:10 NASU).

I realize that stating these values in the "I am" style may seem a bit presumptuous or arrogant. I'm *not* everything that I've written above. But I'm striving to embody those values, and that keeps me humble and ever seeking, two traits missing in some leaders I know. I can never say I've arrived; that could cause me to take shortcuts or expect certain privileges that could lead to defective leadership.

Now how about you? Are you ready to spell out your governing values? Here are some other sample values that I've borrowed from Franklin Covey to help you get started.

- I seek excellence.
- I am competent.

- I serve others.
- I am frugal.
- I am generous.
- I seek truth.
- I am self-sufficient.
- I am innovative.

If you're ready, then follow these simple steps:

1. Set aside two hours.

2. Identify phrases that represent values that have directed your life up to this point.

3. Identify phrases that represent values you wish to incorporate in your life from this point forward.

4. Clarify those phrases and give them definition.

5. Are any of your values harmful to you or others? Do they represent selfish or selfless behavior? You may want to eliminate any that are inconsistent with a lifestyle of love and service (more on this later).

6. Set them in order of priority. Relax! There's no wrong way to do this.

7. Carry them with you. Review them every six months and change as needed.

I trust it's clear how I have used my values to direct my time. Since I value learning, it was an easy decision to go back to school. My work in Africa and in the inner cities of the United States has been directed by my value of reconciliation. Writing, speaking, and seminars came out of my communications value.

There you have what you need to know about the fourth Gold Mine Principle of time management. If this all seems beyond your reach, don't give up. The fifth and final Principle of faith is yet to come in the next section, and it will provide the missing pieces that will help you be purposeful, creative, a goal setter, and an effective manager. Let's turn our attention there now.

GOLD MINE PRINCIPLE #5

FAITH

"I'm Just an Old Chunk of Coal, But I'm Gonna Be a Diamond Someday."

"So that your trust may be in the Lord,
I teach you today, even you." —Proverbs 22:19

Chapter 22

"We'll Be Back" Faith

At this point, you're either fired up and ready to mission-ize, strategize, and organize, or you're about ready to give up. In either case, this last section is designed to provide one final tool you'll need if you're going to mine the gold that's in your life. As I mentioned in the Introduction, I often came away from seminars or books on time management more burdened than when I began. I didn't see how I could possibly do more, and I felt guilty and under pressure that I wasn't doing more. I realized that the one element missing in these presentations was what this section addresses—faith in God.

It's quite possible for you to have read the first four Gold Mine Principles and dismiss them as things that apply to someone else. This section, however, pertains to you and every believer. If you don't apply anything else you've read, you need to pay attention to this section and make it part of your life.

Perhaps you find yourself where many people are: You believe that God can do great things in general, but you're not totally convinced that He can do great things with and through you. Maybe you're painfully aware of your past failures and inadequacies, and those things are weighing you down. You may have even tried some of the things discussed in the previous sections, such as to-do lists and goals, but found no lasting success in implementing them. Even if you did find your purpose, set goals, and express some creativity, you may be thinking that you still wouldn't be able to do great things for the Lord.

That's why this section is subtitled, "I'm Just an Old Chunk of Coal, But I'm Gonna Be a Diamond Someday." That comes from a country western song sung years ago by John Anderson, and it summarizes the mindset you must have if the Lord is to use you for His glory. Abraham, Sarah, Joseph, Moses, David, Esther, Daniel, and Jesus' disciples all started out as "chunks of coal"—raw material in the hands of the Lord. James wrote, "Elijah was a man just like us. He prayed earnestly that it would not rain, and it did not rain on the land for three and a half years" (James 5:17). The prophet Elijah was just like you and me, yet God used him to bring a great deliverance in Israel.

Through the same process that makes diamonds from coal—heat, pressure, and time—these men and women of God became precious gems. They were transformed from ordinary people into extraordinary champions, leaving a legacy for others to follow for thousands of years. When you come right down to it, you're no different. The key element in their transformation wasn't a mission statement, goal sheet, or industrial-sized planner. The key element was their faith in God.

The coal-to-diamonds mentality says, "This is where I am today, but this isn't where I'll be tomorrow," and "God isn't finished with me yet." Coal-to-diamonds faith means that, regardless of how it looks today or how many failures there were yesterday, you've learned to trust, not in your own abilities to make things happen, but in God's ability.

Covey says the second habit of effective people is "Begin with the end in mind." He writes:

> The most fundamental application of "begin with the end in mind" is to begin today with the image, picture, or paradigm of the end of your life as your frame of reference or the criterion by which everything else is examined. . . .By keeping that end clearly in mind, you can make certain that whatever you do on any particular day does not violate the criteria you have defined as supremely important.[1]

The "end in mind" for you is that God isn't finished with you yet.

You should be able to focus on the end and keep it before you so that it will guide how you live and what you say. You can do this through faith that God will finish the work He began in you.

The coal-to-diamonds mentality is the same mentality that Abraham had on Mt. Moriah. He had been instructed to go there by an angel of the Lord and, once there, to sacrifice his son, Isaac. Isaac was the son of promise; Abraham had pinned his hopes for the future on him. But Abraham obediently went to the place the Lord had sent him.

Once he arrived, he spoke these amazing words to his servants who had traveled with him: "Stay here with the donkey while I and the boy go over there. We will worship and then *we will come back to you*" (Genesis 22:5, emphasis added). As far as Abraham was concerned, he was going up that mountain to sacrifice his son. Yet he trusted that God would return that son to him because Isaac was God's promise to Abraham. He said, "We'll be back," and not "I'll be back."

No wonder Abraham is the father of the faithful. He had "we'll-be-back" faith. When it seemed hopeless and he couldn't see his way out, he said, "We'll be back." He didn't ask the servants to pray for him; he didn't seek sympathy or give room for self-pity. He simply said, "We'll be back." In Abraham's mind, he had already sacrificed Isaac; Isaac was dead to him. That's why the writer of Hebrews wrote, "Abraham reasoned that God could raise the dead, and figuratively speaking, he did receive Isaac back from death" (Hebrews 11:19).

If you're Abraham's child, then you need "we'll-be-back" faith, keeping the end in mind, in order to mine the gold in your life. You may have failed at business or ministry before; there may be broken relationships in your past; your financial track record may not be the best. In other words, you may be just an old chunk of coal, but "we'll-be-back" faith says that you'll be a diamond someday through the grace and power of God. Keeping that in mind will cause you to act according to what the end will be and not what today says.

Romans 14:23 states, "Everything that does not come

from faith is sin." I looked up the Greek word for "everything" and made a startling discovery. The word for "everything" in that verse means "everything." Isn't that profound? There are no exceptions. Your purpose, creativity, goals, and time management must start from and be sustained by your faith. If not, they represent your own efforts and will fade away just as every fad or burst of human energy eventually does.

Hebrews 11:6 says, "It's impossible to please God." There's nothing you can say that He doesn't already know; there's nothing you can do that He hasn't seen before or done better; there's nothing you can give Him that He needs; there's nothing you can create that would impress Him. "It's impossible to please God."

Thank God that's not all the verse has to say. In its entirety, it says, "Without faith, it's impossible to please God." Without faith, God is not moved. With it, men and women, some of whom are listed in Hebrews 11, did great things and pleased the Lord in the process.

The most striking thing to me about those people listed in Hebrews 11 is their humanity. None of them was perfect, and some of them had severe character flaws. Yet they operated in faith, and the Lord was pleased with them, so much so that He showcased their lives in this faith "hall of fame" chapter of the Bible.

Think of it. Could Samson (a man with moral problems) be a member in some churches today, let alone a leader? Could Rahab (a prostitute) head up the ladies' prayer meeting? Could Moses (a murderer) lead a denomination today? And how about King David after his adultery and attempted cover-up? Would he have remained king after the modern media had torn him apart through investigative reporting?

In each case, God did not present these heroes for their shortcomings; they were put forth as examples because they were men and women of faith. It was their faith that made the difference, and your faith will make the difference as well.

Faith is vital because it takes you from the realm of the

seen to the realm of the unseen. When you exercise faith, it puts you in touch with reality—not the reality of the five senses, but the reality of the heavenly realm. Faith opens your ears to hear and your eyes to see things from God's perspective, thus freeing you from the limited perspective of this world. Faith also enables you to say, "We'll be back," just like Abraham did.

Paul wrote, "So we fix our eyes not on what is seen, but on what is unseen. For what is seen is temporary, but what is unseen is eternal" (2 Corinthians 4:18). In the next chapter, we'll examine this principle in the life of the prophet Elisha, and then proceed from there to offer suggestions on how to apply your faith in everyday life as you apply the Gold Mine Principles.

Chapter 23

Ears That Hear, Eyes That See

As you know by now, I love the book of Proverbs. Just like other books in the Bible, some of the verses in Proverbs are more difficult to comprehend than others. One such verse for me is found in Proverbs 20:12: "Ears that hear, and eyes that see—the Lord has made them both." For years I wondered what that meant. Common sense told me that the Lord is the Creator of all, including my eyes and ears. And common sense further told me that He made them to see and hear respectively. Why would the writer of Proverbs sense a need to write this seemingly simple verse with an obvious meaning?

As I've studied and meditated on this, I've come to realize some of what Proverbs 20:12 is all about. To help explain it to you, I will use a story found in 2 Kings 6.

> Now the King of Aram was at war with Israel. After conferring with his officers, he said, "I will set up my camp in such and such a place." The man of God sent word to the king of Israel: "Beware of passing that place, because the Arameans are going down there." So the King of Israel checked on the place indicated by the man of God. Time and again Elisha warned the king, so that he was on his guard in such places. This enraged the King of Aram. He summoned his officers and demanded of them,

175

"Will you not tell me which of us is on the side of the king of Israel?" "None of us, my lord the king," said one of his officers, "but Elisha, the prophet who is in Israel, tells the king of Israel the very words you speak in your bedroom" (verses 8-12).

The only logical answer to this situation for the king of Aram was that there was a spy in his midst. Someone was leaking information to the press, so to speak, because the king of Israel always knew what the king of Aram was about to do. There was a spiritual reason, however, behind the king's predicament. There was a man in Israel who had "ears to hear." Elisha didn't pay attention to what everyone else was hearing; he listened to the voice of the Lord. Elisha was using his ears to hear what they were created to hear.

What about you? What do you allow your ears to hear? Do you hear the economic reports and then decide that this isn't a good time to give, invest, or build? When you set your goals, do you let someone else tell you how it can't be done or why you aren't the one to do it? If so, that's not what God made your ears for. He made them to hear His voice and, when you hear it, to march to the beat of His drum.

The story in 2 Kings 6 goes on.

"Go, find out where he is," the king ordered, "so I can send men and capture him." The report came back: "He is in Dothan." Then he sent horses and chariots and a strong force there. They went by night and surrounded the city (2 Kings 6:13-14).

This shows the foolishness of the king of Aram's natural mind! He was just told that the prophet always knew what the king was planning, so the king turned around and contrived another plan just as he had been doing. What made him think that the prophet didn't know about this most recent plot?

So the army went and surrounded the place where Elisha was living, just as they had been commanded. We then read, "When the servant of the man of God got up and went out early the next morning, an army with chariots and horses had surrounded the city. 'Oh, my lord, what shall we do?' the servant asked" (2 Kings 6:15).

Maybe that's your cry as you read this: "Oh, my Lord, the rent is due next Saturday. What shall we do?" "Oh, my Lord. How can I afford a new computer, music lessons, or the investment my business needs?" "Oh, my Lord. Where will the money come from for the ministry or missions?" "Lord, how can I find the time to finish school and work full-time?"

If so, then the Lord would say the same thing to you that He said through the prophet to his servant: "'Don't be afraid,' the prophet answered. 'Those who are with us are more than those who are with them'" (2 Kings 6:16). Perhaps the servant thought, "He doesn't know the situation. I've seen it with my own eyes and it's bad. Let's call the Pentagon or the National Guard or the bank or the counselor. My master has his head in the clouds. He doesn't understand."

Maybe you've done the same thing. Someone has tried to encourage you that your financial situation isn't as bad as you think, yet you've responded with the same words. Perhaps someone has told you that you need a church building, but you know how hard it is to get real estate in your area. Or maybe you've had the idea of opening your own business, but there is "no way" you see to get it started. Even though all those answers may be true, your circumstances don't necessarily need to change. You may need to change and use your eyes for their God-given purpose.

What did Elisha do? Did he talk to his servant? Did he have him read a book or listen to a good sermon on faith? This is what Elisha did: "And Elisha prayed, 'Oh, Lord, open his eyes so he may see.' Then the Lord opened the servant's eyes, and he looked and saw the hills full of horses and chariots of fire all around Elisha" (2 Kings 6:17).

Notice that none of the circumstances changed after Elisha prayed. The foreign armies didn't leave, nor did another army arrive to help. The servant didn't arm himself, nor did bad weather chase the invaders away. The only thing that happened was that the servant's eyes were opened. The prophet understood that the only thing that needed to take place was for his servant's eyes to be opened.

Gold Nugget #18

"Open your eyes,
and you will be satisfied with food."
—Proverbs 20:13 (NAS)

Covey writes a great deal about the concept of paradigms (pronounced **pair**-a-dimes). "A simple way to understand paradigms is to see them as maps.... [A paradigm] is a theory, an explanation, or model of something else."[2] Covey goes on to explain that "to try to change outward attitudes and behaviors does very little good in the long run if we fail to examine the basic paradigms from which those attitudes and behaviors flow."[3]

For instance, prior to Christopher Columbus, most people held the paradigm that the world was flat. Artists drew sketches of ships sailing off the end of the world, and these sketches were consistent with and reinforced the paradigm of the day. A contemporary of the flat-earth paradigm was the one that believed the planets revolved around the earth rather than the sun.

Columbus caused a paradigm shift when he sailed to the New World and proved the earth was round. Copernicus made possible a paradigm shift when he proved the sun to be at the center of the universe as it truly is. People continued to fight the reality of the new paradigms, but their resistance didn't stop the paradigm shifts from taking place.

When you see with eyes of faith, your paradigm or model for reality changes. Elisha's servant experienced a paradigm shift when he saw the chariots and horses that surrounded the army of Aram. You may also only need a paradigm shift rather than a change in your circumstances. Paul wrote to the Ephesian church about their ability to see the unseen:

> I pray also that *the eyes of your heart may be enlightened* in order that you may know the hope to

which he has called you, the riches of his glorious inheritance in the saints, and his incomparably great power for us who believe (Ephesians 1:18-19, emphasis added).

Paul knew what Elisha had known centuries before Paul ever ministered: God wants His people to see things from His perspective. He wants to shift their paradigm from what can be seen with the eyes to the paradigm that comes from the unseen. When they do and begin to trust in that eternal perspective, they have understanding that God can empower them to do great things, regardless of what it looks like in the natural.

Consider this fact in the lives of those mentioned in Hebrews 11 by looking at the following verses:

1. *Now faith is being sure of what we hope for and certain of what we do not see* (11:1). The essence of faith is to be certain not of what you can see but of what you can't see. Enlightened eyes provide certainty about those things that can't be seen with the natural mind.

2. *By faith we understand that the universe was formed at God's command, so that what is seen was not made out of what was visible* (11:3). The source for what is seen is not found in other raw materials that can also be seen. The root of what is seen is in the invisible word of God that brought forth creation.

3. *By faith Noah, when warned about things not yet seen...* (11:7). God spoke to Noah about rain, floods, and an ark, all things that had never been seen before in the natural. Noah put his faith in God's word, even though he had no historical precedent for what the Lord said.

4. *For he was looking forward to the city with foundations* (11:10). What caused Abraham to leave his country and set out for parts unknown? He saw another city, built by God. With that firmly in sight, he set out on a journey that changed the course of mankind.

5. *All these people were still living by faith when they died. They did not receive the things promised; they only saw*

them and welcomed them (11:13). The people of old saw the promises and welcomed them. They didn't actually see them come to pass in history, but when they saw them with their spiritual sight, they felt as if they had them already. They died "in faith" because of what they saw, and God was pleased with them. Seeing things from an eternal perspective in the absence of time may bring the reality of those things much closer than they really are. Yet that doesn't make them any less real.

6. *By faith Moses' parents hid him for three months after he was born, because they saw he was no ordinary child* (11:23). When our son was born, my wife looked at him and said, "Maybe he'll be intelligent." No newborn is beautiful at first due to the trauma of birth. Moses' parents looked at this boy and ignored Pharaoh's edict that he be thrown into the river. They saw the purpose of God on him and it caused them to act differently than the other parents of the day.

7. *He [Moses] was looking ahead to his reward* (11:26). Moses turned his back on his Egyptian inheritance because he saw something else: the reward for the people of God, which was ultimately the Messiah.

8. *By faith he left Egypt, not fearing the king's anger; he persevered because he saw him who is invisible* (11:27). Pharaoh was in Moses' face, intimidating him with threats he could back up with all the power of the Egyptian army. Moses looked right past the one he could see (Pharaoh) to One who can't be seen (the Lord). What he saw in the invisible allowed him to act and eventually pull down the military power of Egypt without an arrow being shot.

9. *Let us fix our eyes on Jesus, the author and perfecter of our faith* (12:2). You are commanded to fix your eyes on the One who is invisible. If you can do that, you will find the source and sustainer of your faith. If you focus on circumstances, your faith will lose its lifeline and perish.

Let me illustrate this further from my own personal experience. Many years ago, we put our house up for sale, but for months nothing happened. We decided that faith requires action (something we will discuss later), so we went out and looked for a new house before the old house was sold. To our surprise, the first house we looked at was the one we fell in love with.

We went home content that we had found our new house, but still nothing was happening on the sale of our old home. So we decided that the next thing to do was to put an offer on the new house, contingent on the sale of our old one.

In the meantime, a family from India submitted an offer on the old home that was so low, we rejected it outright with no counter offer. We were approaching the deadline on the deal, and I prayed one morning and asked God to open my eyes so that I could see what I was missing. That evening my daughter, then just four years old, came running in to tell me that the "Indian family" had just driven by our house. When she said that, I knew that my prayer had been answered. At that very instant, the Lord opened my eyes to see that the people who had submitted the only offer we had received were still interested. I had rejected their offer because I thought it was too low. I realized then and there that I was to take their offer and trust the Lord for the money we would still need to move into our new home.

I called my realtor that night and told him to make the best deal he could. Just 36 hours before our deadline on the new house offer, we sold our house. Of course, we were still $10,000 short of what we needed to close on the new home. God had opened my eyes, however, and I was trusting Him. Two weeks later, we closed on that new house. Someone unexpectedly loaned us the $10,000 at a low interest rate. We paid that money back and enjoyed our new home for five years, selling it after we relocated to Orlando, Florida. The Lord had used my four- year-old to open my eyes and I saw things from His perspective. The rest was worked out in the natural as we relied on Him for the provision.

God will do the same for you. He wants you to have eyes that see and ears that hear, just as He created them. As we close this chapter, let's touch on one more verse. Perhaps you've quoted it or heard someone preach about it. It's found in Ephesians

3:20 and is most often quoted, "Now to him who is able to do immeasurably more than all we ask or imagine." If you've ever quoted that verse in that way, you've made a serious mistake! God is *not* able to do immeasurably more than all you ask or imagine because He is not in the "immeasurably-more" business without having the last part of that verse included, "according to his power that is at work within us." If there's no power working in you, then God's power is limited, not by design, but by His choice.

What energizes the power within you? It's the vision you have of what God can do that comes when you use your eyes to see and ears to hear. That vision of the "end in mind" allows you to trust the Lord to do what He said or showed you He would do, regardless of what is happening around you. God is faithful and powerful, but your faith in Him releases His power to act on your behalf.

Gold Nugget #19

"Where there is no vision,
the people are unrestrained."
—Proverbs 29:18 (NAS)

Before you read the next chapter, ask the Lord to open your ears and eyes. Ask Him to show you what you haven't seen that can make the difference in your life. Maybe you need to stop praying for your situation to change, and start praying for your heart to change. Or maybe you just need to have your eyes or ears opened. Perhaps you can't see yourself fulfilling your purpose, being creative, or achieving lofty goals. You may be saying, "I'm disorganized and that's how I'll always be." If so, then you need to change your personal paradigm.

There's no better way to change your heart or paradigm than to clarify your vision of reality from the Lord's perspective. Once you've done that, move on to the next chapter that will show you how to preserve your faith so that you can see the object of your faith fulfilled.

Chapter 24

How Can I Know for Sure?

Most people want certainty where the things of God are concerned. One of the great fears I hear regularly is that people don't want to miss the Lord or get ahead of Him. The question I'm most often asked when it comes to operating in faith is: How can I be sure it's the Lord so that I'm not walking in presumption? You may be concerned about that same issue because you've seen others so sure they were walking in faith, only to be disappointed when what they had faith for never came to pass. When that happens, people are embarrassed, the Lord's reputation is damaged, and people suffer. Those examples may be preventing you from acting in bold faith because you fear ending up like those disappointed people.

What's more, people have read Hebrews 11:1, which states that faith is "the assurance of things hoped for, the conviction of things unseen" (NASB). They want to know how they can have conviction of spiritual things that cannot be seen. That would include the Gold Mine Principles like purpose, creativity, and goals. I cannot blame anyone for seeking the assurance of faith when we are dealing with such important issues in the will of God.

I've had to work through these issues myself, for as a pastor, I saw my share of faith adventures gone awry. And to be truthful, I've had a few myself. Yet over the years I've answered two related questions that have helped me answer the question, "How can I be sure it's the Lord directing me?"

A fellow pastor asked me the first question while we were having lunch. He asked me, "Why do you think there are counterfeit $20 bills?" I thought for a while but couldn't give him a satisfactory answer. He finally answered his own question by saying, "Because there are real $20 bills." No one is going to go to the trouble of counterfeiting something that has no value. Counterfeiters imitate the real thing in hopes of passing off the fake as real.

Just because I know there are counterfeit $20 bills doesn't mean I refuse to accept any $20 bills at all. If I'm that concerned about getting a fake $20, I would simply take precautions to make sure that what I get is real. If a phony bill was to get by me, I would accept it as loss and try to be more careful. But if I became so paranoid that what I'm getting may be fake, I could pass up the real thing by being too cautious.

That's how it is with faith. Of course there is counterfeit faith in circulation. It's there to discourage the people of God from operating in real and vibrant faith. Just because some (even you) have accepted a fake at one time or another doesn't mean that you should reject all faith. Treat the mistakes like you would treat that fake $20 bill: Learn from it and be better prepared to distinguish the real from the fake.

Answering that question helped me see that there are no sure things in life or faith. I saw that my desire to know for sure before I would ever act was unrealistic and presumptuous. Abraham didn't understand it all before he left his homeland, and once he started, he made some mistakes along the way. Fortunately, he didn't give up on ever having an Isaac just because he had fathered an Ishmael. God is bigger than my mistakes, and is able to work with my mistakes if my heart is right.

The second question that helped me answer "How can I be sure?" was asked by a fellow pastor in a message on the family. He challenged me, "Because there's divorce, do you stop holding out marriage as God's standard for the family?" After some thought, I concluded the answer was no. I've seen some marriages end in divorce, yet I've continued to give marriage counseling, perform weddings, and do all I could to uphold the family. I've mourned the divorces, but I haven't given up on marriage.

I concluded that's how you should also treat faith. Just because imperfect people have applied it imperfectly at times doesn't mean that you should be afraid or hesitant to walk in faith yourself. Hold onto the truth that "without faith it's impossible to please God" and walk in it, knowing that you are imperfect and will never have perfect knowledge or understanding.

With that in mind, you won't be shocked or allow your faith to be shipwrecked when having to make mid-course changes or adjustments if you understand the Lord and your own motives more clearly. In other words, you'll be like the father who told Jesus, "I do believe; help me overcome my unbelief" (Mark 9:24).

This father admitted his imperfection, including his unbelief, and Jesus still healed his boy. His unbelief didn't cause the Lord to shun him or leave him until his faith was perfect. Instead, the man's honest admission of his human weakness still moved the Lord to act on his behalf.

While there is always the danger that you're moving in your own strength or understanding, there are two things that will help you avoid the pain of faith that is presumptuous or off course. These two things can also help you answer the question, "How can I be sure?" The first is to realize that the agenda for your faith rests in God's hands. The second is that you must prepare your heart to receive the word of the Lord, the foundation for your faith. Let's address both these issues separately.

The agenda for your faith rests in God, so you don't have to work up one for yourself. You don't have to ask, "What will I believe the Lord for today?" This also means that you aren't free to decide what you want to have, what you want to be, and how you want to get there. All those things should have their beginning in the Lord, and you should enter into their reality after He has made them clear to you.

And that's good news. God is the initiator or author of your faith. It's not up to you to work up or work out your faith. God has given each person a measure of faith, and He will show you where you need to exercise that faith. When God wants to make something clear, He is more than able to do it. All you have to be is receptive and willing to follow through.

That is why I work with people to take their thoughts and ideas seriously and not to be too quick to write them off as "not from the Lord." God will use your thoughts to guide your actions and direction, but those thoughts must be accepted in faith. If you pray, "God I will do Your will; what is it?" and then you have a chance meeting or receive an unexpected phone call, either of which is related to your prayer, then you must at least consider in faith that God has answered your prayer and not dismiss either as random.

On May 18, 1973, I met the Lord through a simple but profound conversion. I was raised Catholic and had studied to be a priest for five years before leaving to pursue other interests. On May 19, I knew that the Lord was saying to me, "You're going to leave your church, go into full-time ministry and preach, and give your life to My service."

How did I know? I'm not sure. Those were not things I really wanted to do or had ever considered doing, nor were they something I was anticipating. But I couldn't shake those thoughts from that day on. God had communicated with me, and it was up to me to put my faith in what He showed me that day. The ministry became part of my faith agenda. How sure was I? I was certain that the Lord had spoken to me. Did I have times of doubt? Definitely! During those times, all I could do was put my faith in what I believed I had heard from the Lord. The rest was up to Him. Others who have been called to the ministry can share their own callings, and some are certainly more dramatic than mine. My point is that I placed my faith in that call and hung onto it through good times and bad. And there were plenty of bad times.

I didn't step into my own pulpit until 16 years later. There were times when I was so far away from a pulpit that I didn't see how the gap could ever be closed. All I had was that word from the Lord. And there were times during those 16 years when I hoped that it wouldn't come true. But every time I would get low, the Lord would send a messenger, a verse, or a reminder, and His promise would be activated in me once again—I would one day be in His service.

This is the same situation in which Abraham found himself. While he wanted a child, it was the Lord who initiated the promise of a son. Abraham didn't make it up; God spoke it to him.

There were times when it seemed like the promise had failed. Abraham had even tried to assist God by getting Sarah's maid pregnant. Even in the midst of his failure, however, the word remained in effect. Then, when Abraham was 100 years old, the word of the Lord came true, and he had a son.

Abraham didn't "name and claim" a child. He didn't decide one day that the Lord owed him a son because he saw so many others who had one or more. You don't ever have to do that either. God spoke to Abraham, and that became the foundation for his faith that he would have a son. God will speak to you, too, and your only responsibility is to hear and obey. Abraham's faith agenda began and ended with God. Yours does too as you trust in Jesus, "the author and perfecter of our faith."

Now when I say that the Lord will speak to you, you may again be concerned how God will speak, and whether you'll be able to hear. Don't worry. God is able to make clear whatever He wants to say. He may use circumstances, another person, a verse of Scripture, a still, small inner voice, or any combination of these to confirm His word for your life. Even then you may have doubt. What better time to exercise what faith you do have!

I trust you can see the relevance of this for the Gold Mine Principles. People will ask, "How do you know that's your purpose?" You asked God, had faith, and then trust that what you saw or understood is the answer to your quest. "How do you know what book to write or picture to paint?" You know by faith, for you did not have 100 ideas, you had just one or two, and acted on those ideas. "Is that the right goal for your life at this time?" You have been thinking about it for three years, it won't go away, so in faith, you accept it as something you are supposed to do.

Having established that the Lord will set your faith agenda, the second issue you must address is that you must prepare your heart to receive God's word. Faith doesn't have to be dramatic with lightning flashes and the voice of God blasting from the mountaintop. Faith can and often does come as you prepare your heart, a heart that is often ill-equipped to do business with God.

One of Jesus' disciples was named Thomas, and we know him today as "Doubting Thomas." When he was told that the Lord had risen from the dead, Thomas' response was as follows: "Unless I see the nail marks in his hands and put my finger where the nails were, and put my hand into his side, I will not believe" (John 20:25). Thomas persisted in this hardness of heart for one week, until the Lord showed up to provide the evidence he demanded:

> A week later his disciples were in the house again, and Thomas was with them. Though the doors were locked, Jesus came and stood among them and said, "Peace be with you!" Then he said to Thomas, "Put your finger here; see my hands. Reach out your hand and put it into my side. Stop doubting and believe." Thomas said to him, "My Lord and my God!" Then Jesus told him, "Because you have seen me, you have believed; blessed are those who have not seen and yet have believed" (John 20:26-29).

We should not be too hard on Thomas, for Jesus confronted all the disciples after His resurrection concerning the same problem: hardness of heart: "Later Jesus appeared to the Eleven as they were eating; he rebuked them for their lack of faith and their stubborn refusal to believe those who had seen him after he had risen" (Mark 16:14). It is obvious from this confrontation that this hardness was something the disciples had permitted, even cultivated, and the Lord indicated that this was unacceptable.

The writer of Hebrews included this admonition in his letter:

So, tried me and for forty years saw what I did. That is why I was angry with that generation, and I said, 'Their hearts are always going astray, and they have not known my ways.' So I declared on oath in my anger, 'They shall never enter my rest.'" *See to it, brothers, that none of you has a sinful, unbelieving heart that turns away from the living God* (Hebrews 3:7-12, emphasis added).

The writer didn't suggest that perhaps the people needed to consider not having a "sinful, unbelieving heart." He *commanded* them not to allow one to develop. And it seems that the writer especially cautioned you to be careful not to harden your heart "if you hear his voice." When the Lord speaks, you can choose to accept and act, or to ignore and stay put. The decision is yours; very often that decision will be dictated by the condition of our heart.

There are many ways to keep your heart in good shape. Maintain a vibrant prayer life; read the Word of God regularly and seek understanding. Choose topics and study what the word of God has to say about them in depth. Memorizing Scripture verses is a good way to store the Word in your heart.

I also carry maintain a brief journal of significant things the Lord has shown me over the years. I refer to this list in times of discouragement, and it refreshes me by allowing me to remember truths the Lord has shown me from His word or through experience. With technology as it is today, carrying reminders of God's work and words to you should not be too difficult! There are others who have made a practice of keeping a daily journal that chronicles their walk with the Lord. Every now and then they read their journal entries, which reminds them of the Lord's faithfulness and stimulates their faith.

You may also want to consider keeping your own journal, using your time-management system or your technology for regular entries. But at least have a file or some other means to maintain those special insights the Lord has given you.

I've also found fasting to be an excellent practice that helps keep your heart soft and pliable in God's hands. You may want to choose a regular day on which you fast and also block out on your calendar several days every six months or so when you just give up eating and spend that time with the Lord.

Finally, asking the Lord to show you the condition of your heart should be a regular prayer. The psalmist wrote, "Search me, O God, and know my heart; test me and know my anxious thoughts. See if there is any offensive way in me, and lead me in the way everlasting" (Psalm 139:23-24). God knows the condition of your heart, and can keep you aware of what's there as well. The key is to ask Him to do so.

When it comes to faith, everyone must answer the question, "How can I be sure?" While you can never be 100% certain, there are steps you can take to make your margin for error smaller and smaller as you walk in faith. First of all, **relax**. Jesus is the author and initiator of your faith. Then **prepare your heart** to receive the word of the Lord and work to keep it from hardening once you've heard. If you **make your best efforts**, God won't abandon you. He'll meet you where you are because anyone who comes to Him "must believe that he exists and that he rewards those who earnestly seek him" (Hebrews 11:6). With that in mind, let's move on to define the final steps to be taken if you're to make the transition from coal to diamonds.

Chapter 25

Walk in What You See

Faith takes you from the realm of the seen to the realm of the unseen. It causes you to walk and act according to invisible circumstances that sometimes would seem to warrant doing the exact opposite of what you can see would dictate. If the bills are due and you have a few dollars, the last thing you should do in the natural is to give that money away. Yet, when you move from the realm of the seen to the unseen, that may be the very thing you need and choose to do.

You may feel that you must deny reality, not even mentioning what is happening around you, if you are to have your faith rewarded. This has led some people to deny symptoms of sickness, ignore financial problems, or make desperate faith confessions to try and escape difficult situations, and to prove they have faith. But walking in what you see in the invisible doesn't require you to do any of that.

Gold Nugget #20

"A fool's eyes wander to the ends of the earth."
—Proverbs 17:24

Paul wrote about Abraham in the epistle to the Romans, describing Abraham's struggle in becoming a father. He wrote,

Against all hope, Abraham in hope believed and

so became the father of many nations, just as it had been said to him, "So shall your offspring be." Without weakening in his faith, he faced the fact that his body was as good as dead—since he was about a hundred years old—and that Sarah's womb was also dead. Yet he did not waver through unbelief regarding the promise of God, but was strengthened in his faith and gave glory to God, being fully persuaded that God had power to do what he had promised. This is why "it was credited to him as righteousness" (Romans 4:18-22).

Abraham didn't deny the reality of his situation. His body was dead and so was Sarah's. He didn't tell people that he was alive, that in faith he was as good as a 20-year-old. Abraham said, "I'm dead."

But Abraham is our father in the faith because he didn't stop there. He chose to focus on the unseen promise of God without wavering. If someone asked Abraham, "How are you going to have a son?" He probably replied, "I don't know. I'm dead, but God's alive. And if He's alive, then anything can happen." He didn't make silly statements trying to prove to people that he and Sarah still had some supernatural ability to produce a child. He faced the facts—he was dead. He lived in a more powerful fact, however. God was able to do what He had promised, and that saved the day.

I previously referred to my 16-year wait for a pulpit. I didn't use those 16 years desperately seeking a pulpit position or maneuvering to get a chance to preach. God had me boxed in, and there was nowhere to go. But I didn't waste those years. I used them by walking in the greater truth that God had shown me—I was a preacher, and one day, regardless of what it seemed like, I would preach.

So I used those years to get ready. I studied as many preachers as I could. I wrote my own sermons and then preached to myself in the car. I preached to my kids, my wife, my home group (which sometimes numbered four people, including my wife and me), and our hamster.

While I wasn't preaching, I would visualize myself preaching. In my mind, I worked out a preaching style and philosophy that helped me discover what I would say and how I would say it when I got the chance.

Covey refers to this ability to visualize when he writes,

Through imagination, we can visualize the uncreated worlds of potential that lie within us. Through conscience, we can come in contact with universal laws or principles with our own singular talents and avenues of contribution, and with the personal guidelines within which we can most effectively develop them. Combined with self-awareness, these two endowments empower us to write our own script. Because we already live with many scripts that have been handed to us, the process of writing our own script is actually more a process of "rescripting" or paradigm shifting.[4]

When the call came for me to pastor a church, I was ready because I had walked in the reality of the unseen. I chose (and sometimes forced myself) to ignore circumstances and prepare according to God's agenda. I held the paradigm that God's word made me a preacher, whether I was preaching at that particular season in my life or not.

When I finally "arrived," I had material ready to preach and knew what kind of preacher I wanted to be. When my call reached its fulfillment, I was glad I had prepared myself according to the vision I had of the unseen and not according to the "reality" of my current circumstances.

I briefly touched on how faith affects your speech earlier in this book; this is a good time to address that more fully. The book of Proverbs has plenty of verses that speak about the tongue. James' epistle, sometimes called the Proverbs of the New Testament, also has much to say about your speech. You may be asking yourself, "What is appropriate to say when I'm walking in faith and everything around me seems to make my faith foolish?" At times like that, you simply say what the Lord has already said or shown you. And if you don't know what to say, don't say anything.

For instance, when people would ask me what I felt God had called me to do before I ever went to pastor the church, I would tell them "to preach." They would then ask me all the normal questions: Where are you preaching now? Did you go to seminary? If you're not preaching, why aren't you? Shouldn't you get a pulpit somewhere?

I would reply that the Lord had called me to preach and that He would open a place for me. I further explained that I had never applied for a job in my life and didn't feel that I should start applying for a church position. I was where God had me for that season, and I was content to be there. Beyond that, there wasn't much else I could say. Some didn't understand, but I kept right on saying that God had called me to preach, because He had. Just because I wasn't preaching at the time didn't negate that fact.

Gold Nugget #21

"From the fruit of his mouth a man's stomach is filled; with the harvest from his lips he is satisfied. The tongue has the power of life and death, and those who love it will eat its fruit."
—Proverbs 18:20-21

I'm sure some didn't understand either when Abram changed his name. Can you picture this fictitious scene at the name-change bureau? Abram, whose name meant "exalted father," came to the clerk and announced his intent to change his name. When the clerk asked him what his new name would be, he announced it to be Abraham, which means "father of a multitude."

Intrigued by such a name change, maybe the clerk asked Abraham a logical question: "How many children do you have?" to which Abraham had to respond, "None!" At that point, the clerk probably just rolled his eyes and wondered what kind of religious "kook" he was dealing with, who would change his name to "father of a multitude" though he was old and without children.

The point is that Abraham changed his name, not because he decided to do so, but because the Lord *told* him to do it. God wanted Abraham and everyone around him to make a faith statement each time they said that name. There are times when you can and must say what you know to be true, *not to try to make something happen,* but to acknowledge that in God's time something will happen.

Because they were people of faith, those mentioned in Hebrews 11 had seen only by faith what they proclaimed. For instance, "By faith Jacob, when he was dying, blessed each of Joseph's sons" (Hebrews 11:21) even though he died in Egypt. It's written about Joseph that "when his end was near, [he] spoke about the exodus of the Israelites from Egypt and gave instructions about his bones" (Hebrews 11:22). Both Jacob and Joseph acknowledged the fact that their people would return to their land someday by making a faith confession. God had said it and they could, too.

Paul referred to this same principle when he wrote, "It is written: 'I believed, therefore I have spoken.' With that same spirit of faith, we also believe and therefore speak" (2 Corinthians 4:13). What is it that you believe and, because you do, can't keep to yourself?

And finally, when you are firm in what you have seen, it's then time to take action. James wrote, "Faith by itself, if it is not accompanied by action, is dead" (James 2:17). Faith is more than adhering to a correct doctrine. The demons believe in the Trinity, beholding it regularly, but that fact hasn't changed them one bit.

You must shift any paradigm you're holding that says your faith is what you believe doctrinally. Your faith must translate into action or it's not faith at all. It's not giving mental assent to the doctrine of the Trinity that makes you a Christian. It's what you do because of your faith in the Trinity that makes you a Christian.

In an earlier chapter, I told of our adventure in purchasing a new home before we ever sold our old home. I had to ask myself each step of the way, "What can I do at this moment? What can I do so that I've done all I can, leaving the rest up to the Lord?"

My faith that I would one day preach also required me to do something. I chose to get ready to preach as opposed to applying for associate pastor positions. My point is that faith always leads to action. Not one hero of the faith in Hebrews 11 was a great theologian. Instead, each one knew how to act on his or her faith. Let's look at the people mentioned in that chapter and see how they acted on their faith to God.

Abel	offered a better sacrifice
Noah	built an ark
Abraham	left his home, made a home in a new place, offered Isaac
Isaac	blessed Jacob and Esau
Jacob	blessed his sons and worshiped God
Joseph	gave instructions about his bones
Moses	left Egypt and kept the Passover
Israel	passed through the Red Sea; marched and the walls fell
Rahab	hid the spies

In addition, we are told that other people,

> ...through faith conquered kingdoms, administered justice, and gained what was promised; who shut the mouths of lions, quenched the fury of the flames, and escaped the edge of the sword; whose weakness was turned to strength; and who became powerful in battle and routed foreign armies (Hebrews 11:33-34).

Faith requires action and those who took action in faith are mentioned and honored in the word of God in spite of their weakness and sin. Those who move in faith are still honored by the Lord, and He works with and through them in spite of their weakness and failure.

I'm not only talking about faith for your car payment, shoes for your children, and a roof over your head—the necessities of life. I'm talking about faith to apply the Gold Mine Principles more fully in your life, or faith to fulfill the Great Commission, through which the Church is to disciple the nations. How can you have faith for Africa or Asia if you can't exercise faith for the simple things? How will you trust the Lord for the millions of dollars it will take to publish Bibles in the thousands of dialects currently without the Word of God if you can't trust Him for the $25 monthly commitment you've made to help support your church's missionary to India?

If you believe in Jesus' resurrection, and I'm sure you do, then you're in for an adventure! Anyone who has faith to believe that God took a three-day-old dead body and infused it with life can have faith for anything! The same Spirit that raised a dead man back to life dwells in you, helping you in ways you can't see or understand. He's there in you, and together you can do great things.

With that fact established, you can find and accomplish your purpose. In faith, you can express your creativity like a bird sings every morning in the forest. In faith, you can set goals and in faith you can see them fulfilled "beyond all you can ask or think." Like Joshua, you can have faith that God will help you maximize your use of time and help you to do more with the time you have. You can take your faith to your desk, garage, or kitchen and trust the Lord to show you how to organize it and keep it ordered.

John wrote his first epistle and penned these words:

For everyone born of God overcomes the world. This is the victory that has overcome the world, even our faith. Who is it that overcomes the world? Only he who believes that Jesus is the Son of God (1 John 5:4-5).

You can overcome the world and its obstacles through faith. Someone wrote, "It's not the greatness of my faith that moves mountains, but my faith in the greatness of God."

With that in mind, move on to the last chapter where you'll find some practical assignments to further help you walk in faith that will please God and perhaps change the world.

Chapter 26
"Action!"

So now that you've decided to walk according to the unseen and act on your faith, where can you go from here? To give you some direction, I've included a few activities that have nurtured my faith over the years. I offer them to you in hopes that they will spur you to love and good deeds as the Bible commands.

1. Is your giving all it can be?

If you keep financial records, check to see what percentage of your income you gave away last year. Are you satisfied with that amount? If not, what percent would you like to give away this year? When you decide that, then determine how much you must give away each month to achieve that percentage. I've found that my giving is the most practical and accurate indicator of my faith, and I try to keep the total amount I give significantly above a ten-percent tithe.

I never give offerings based on my bills. In other words, I try to pray and give what I feel the Lord is directing me to give. When He shows me the amount, I give it without worrying whether that money should have been used for something else. If the Lord directs me to give money today that I was saving for a bill three days later, I always try to give today. Often I will consult with my wife, and more often than not, she will confirm the exact amount I was considering to give. If she suggests an amount greater than I was anticipating, then I give that greater amount.

I stress that we give only after consulting the Lord and give the amount He directs us to give. It's irresponsible and presumptuous to blindly write checks for God's work when you have bills due. I've found that only on occasion has He directed me to give money "beyond my means"—money that was to have been used to pay something else. When He has so directed, He has also provided to cover the need created by that unusual offering. At the same time, I've never tried to keep something in the bank as a cushion against the unexpected when the Lord has directed to give that money away.

The writer of Ecclesiastes advised you to "cast your bread upon the waters, for after many days you will find it again" (Ecclesiastes 11:1). Cast your bread regularly and abundantly and watch for the return to come in due season. Your faith will be rewarded.

Whenever I've gotten discouraged over my finances, I've pressed into God's Word for comfort and encouragement. Over the years, the following have been my favorite verses where finances are concerned:

- "Let us not become weary in doing good, for at the proper time we will reap a harvest if we do not give up" (Galatians 6:9).

- You need to persevere so that when you have done the will of God, you will receive what he has promised. For in just a very little while, "He who is coming will come and will not delay. But my righteous one will live by faith. And if he shrinks back, I will not be pleased with him." But we are not of those who shrink back and are destroyed, but of those who believe and are saved (Hebrews 10:36-39).

- "Give, and it will be given to you. A good measure, pressed down, shaken together and running over, will be poured into your lap. For with the measure you use, it will be measured to you" (Luke 6:38).

- Remember this: Whoever sows sparingly will also reap sparingly, and whoever sows generously will also reap generously (2 Corinthians 9:6).

- And my God will meet all your needs according to his

glorious riches in Christ Jesus (Philippians 4:19).

Money is something that you handle almost every day. It's therefore a pertinent indicator of your faith and how you're putting it into action.

2. Your life's purpose and goals

Section One led you through a discussion and exercises to help you identify your life's purpose. Assuming that you can now summarize it in one sentence, what do you have faith to accomplish with that purpose? What goals have you set that will be accomplished only through God's power released by your faith? In Section Two, we looked at creativity. Are you accepting your creative thoughts as possibly being from God and acting on them?

To help you with this, why don't you think about what you would do if money and time weren't factors. Would you start a business? If you answer yes, then how much money would that business make in its first ten years? How many would you employ? How much money would you give to the Lord's work?

My own faith goals included plans to start a ministry called "Gold Mine Development Corporation." I wanted to see thousands released to function in their God-given purpose and then equipped and trained to be efficient and organized. I did start it in 2001, only to rename it a few years later when I kept getting emails from mining concerns seeking partnerships! Today, PurposeQuest Incorporated has continued to do the work that I envisioned for Gold Mine Development.

After that, I wanted to see those same Gold Mine Principles taught and applied in other nations for which I carry a concern. That desire led me to form PurposeQuest International, a nonprofit entity that raises money for orphans, widows, and Gold Mine Principles teaching in Africa. I still set goals for my ongoing education, the number of books I would like to write, and some "chaotic" situations to which I would like to create order in my lifetime. I have no idea how some of these will come about, but faith doesn't require me to have all the answers before I plan or act.

I have written these goals out and review them regularly. Some of them are far from being a reality, but then so was my getting a pulpit at one time. God worked that out, and He will work these out as well. If they never come to pass, I plan on dying in faith, having seen them and welcomed them from afar.

3. Your Bible study

I've never been very keen on reading the Bible straight through. I've done it a few times, but I've had much greater success studying topics and individuals in an in-depth manner. I would like to suggest some faith studies that have added a great deal to my understanding and ability to apply my faith. After all, if faith requires action, then maybe your first action step should be to study faith (but remember, don't study just to learn; study so you can swing into action).

A. **Read the four gospels and record in your journal everything Jesus said using the words faith and believe.** Record your thoughts on these verses, and group them as they fit together. You may want to highlight those verses with one particular color in your study Bible. From there, you can do the same for Paul's epistles, John's epistles, and James' letter. A comprehensive understanding of faith will come only when you get a complete overview, not just singling out your favorite verses.

B. **Do a thorough study of Hebrews 11.** Assign some of the names mentioned in that chapter some space in your time management journal, and then study their lives in the Bible. Keep notes of what you discover on those pages. Study each one with a view toward answering why they qualified to be listed in Hebrews 11. Single out one or two who are particularly relevant to your life and calling, and make them the object of more intense, long-term study.

C. **Based on these studies, reflect on and journal the changes you can make in your life.** Write down the thoughts you have from this and discuss them with your pastor, mentor, spouse, and children. Remember, faith leads to action, so study with an eye toward doing something.

As we close, be reminded that nothing is too difficult for

God. He is in the business of doing the impossible. With that in mind, have faith! No matter how bleak it looks, God can come through with the unexpected and miraculous. So dream and plan accordingly. Put your hand in God's and hold on for the ride of your life. As you do, you'll join with the heroes of faith and earn your own place in the ongoing rendition of Hebrews 11, a chapter that is still being written for the people of God who have faith.

I hope by now that you are convinced there is gold in your life. Your purpose, creativity, and the goals you set are of great worth, more valuable than any riches this life can offer. Consequently, your time should be invested in those things that are the most meaningful for you and that will yield the greatest return. To avoid wasting time, you should organize your world so that you can give yourself to the highest priority at any given time.

Yet as I've stressed again and again, it's all for naught if you don't have faith, for "without faith it is impossible to please God" (Hebrews 11:6). Trust God for great things, just as the apostles did in Acts 6. Opportunities abound for those who walk in purpose and faith. May the Lord bless you on your faith journey, and may you hear those wonderful words, "Well done, good and faithful servant" at the end of the road.

Notes

Introduction

[1]Richard Nelson Bolles, *The 1994 What Color is Your Parachute?* (Ten Speed Press, 1994), page 435.
[2]Ibid., 447.

Section One

[1]Stephen R. Covey, *The Seven Habits of Highly Effective People* (New York: Simon & Shuster Inc., 1989), page 60.
[2]Peter Drucker, *The Effective Executive* (New York: Harper & Row, 1966), pages 52, 70.
[3]Bolles, *The 1994 What Color is Your Parachute?*, page 438.
[4]*Christian History*, Issue 31, page 3.
[5]*Christian History*, Issue 31, page 34.
[6]*Christian History*, Issue 31, page 4.
[7]Bolles, *The 1994 What Color is Your Parachute?*, page 436.

Section Two

[1]Julia Cameron, *The Right to Write* (New York: Tarcher/Putnam, 1998), page 101.

Section Three

[1]Covey, *The 7 Habits*, page 43.
[2]David Collins, *Man's Slave Becomes God's Scientist: George Washington Carver* (Milford, Michigan: Mott Media, 1981), pages 105-106.
[3]*Remarks by Paul H. O'Neill*, Alcoa Organizational Meeting, August 9, 1991.
[4]Covey, *The 7 Habits*, page 71.

[5]Robert Schuller, *Tough-Minded Faith for Tender-Hearted People* (Toronto: Bantam Books, 1983), page 110.

Section Four

[1]*Bits and Pieces*, April 1, 1993, page 7.
[2]*Christian History*, Issue 29, Volume X, No. 1, pages 2-3.
[3]Covey, *The 7 Habits*, pages 153-154.
[4]Peter Drucker, *Management Challenges for the 21st Century* (New York: Harper Collins, 1999), page 179.
[5]Alec MacKenzie, *The Time Trap* (New York: American Management Association, 1990), page 3.
[6]Merril E. and Donna N. Douglass, *Manage Your Time, Your Work, Yourself* (New York: American Management Association, 1993), page 109.

Section Five

[1]Covey, *The 7 Habits*, page 98.
[2]Ibid., page 23.
[3]Ibid., page 28.

Epilogue

Revising this book has been a great experience, and I hope it was the same for you as you read through it. It was great from my end because it caused me to review these concepts I had written about and taught over the last 25 years. I realized as I edited and reviewed that I was just as committed to these Principles now as I was then, but in a more mature and comprehensive way. My teaching on each subject has matured and is seasoned with more reality and life experience that I trust has only made their impact stronger and more relevant.

This revision also took me down memory lane, reminding me of what a great ride it's been with these Gold Mine Principles as partners. I have taught and written about them thousands of times, but the most meaningful part of the journey has been their personal applications in my own life. I know that these Principles are effective in large part because I have been diligent to apply them. They have taken me to many countries, allowed me to make some wonderful friends, and equipped me to write and speak with authority on all five Principles. I have had the privilege of hearing from many who also applied the Principles and heard their amazing and exciting results.

Finally, this work has confirmed the importance of the Gold Mine Principles in today's world. They are even more important than when I first began teaching them, for modern times have presented people with more options of how to invest their time, and opportunities to be creative and purposeful. In the face of so many things that one *can* do, it is more important than ever to identify what it is that one *should* do. Paying attention to the Gold Mine Principles will help anyone be more focused and productive in a good way, for purpose and creativity are fueled by joy, and Nehemiah 8:10 says that "the joy of the Lord is your strength."

I don't know how many days I have left on earth, and it may only be a few for all I know. As I conclude, I want to devote my remaining days to developing and disseminating the gospel of the Gold Mine Principles. I hope that includes travel and teaching, but I want to express as much of what I know and learn through writing. Speaking slots pass away quickly, but writing lasts forever—or at least outlasts the life span of the writer. I have often told audiences that my books may become more popular after I'm gone, or God can place them in my coffin and bury all of us. It's up to Him. Every writer, however, writes in faith that someone, somewhere will find our work, read it, and benefit from it. It is my **goal** to continue to use my **time** to **creatively** write about **purpose**, exercising **faith** that God will use what I produce for His purpose. I'm not sure I have ever produced a sentence with all five Gold Mine Principles in it. That would be a good place to end this revision.

You can follow my purpose journey through my Monday Memo and blog sites, listed at the end of this book, or you can read some of my other books for more stories and testaments to the power of purpose. I always enjoy hearing a story of a purpose journey, so feel free to write me through any of the social media to which I regularly contribute and through which I communicate. I pray that God will help you apply what you have just read, and will help you find the gold mine in your life as you dig. Happy digging!

About the Author

John Stanko was born in Pittsburgh, Pennsylvania. After graduating from St. Basil's Prep School in Stamford, Connecticut, he attended Duquesne University where he received his bachelor's and master's degrees in economics in 1972 and 1974 respectively.

Since then, John has served as an administrator, teacher, consultant, author, and pastor in his professional career. He holds a second master's degree in pastoral ministries, and earned his doctorate in pastoral ministries from Liberty Theological Seminary in Houston, Texas in 1995. He recently completed a doctor of ministry degree at Reformed Presbyterian Theological Seminary in Pittsburgh.

John has taught extensively on the topics of time management, life purpose, and organization, and has conducted leadership and purpose training sessions throughout the United States and in 32 countries. He is also certified to administer the DISC and other related personality assessments as well as the Natural Church Development profile for churches. In 2006, he earned the privilege to facilitate for The Pacific Institute of Seattle, a leadership and personal development program, and for The Leadership Circle, a provider of cultural and executive 360-degree profiles. He has authored 28 books and written for many publications around the world.

John founded a personal and leadership development company, called PurposeQuest, in 2001 and today travels the world to speak, consult and inspire leaders and people everywhere. From 2001-2008, he spent six months a year in Africa and still enjoys visiting and working on that continent, while teaching for Geneva College's Masters of Organizational Leadership and the Center for Urban Biblical Ministry in his hometown of Pittsburgh, Pennsylvania. John has been married for more than 40 years to Kathryn Scimone Stanko, and they have two adult children and one grandchild. In 2009, John was appointed the administrative pastor for discipleship at Allegheny Center Alliance Church on the North Side of Pittsburgh where he served for five years. Most recently, John founded Urban Press, a publishing company designed to tell stories of the city, from the city, and to the city.

Keep in Touch
with John Stanko

www.purposequest.com

www.johnstanko.us

www.stankobiblestudy.com

www.stankomondaymemo.com

or via email at johnstanko@gmail.com

John also does extensive relief and community development
work in Kenya. You can see some of his projects at
www.purposequest.com/contributions

PurposeQuest International
PO Box 8882
Pittsburgh, PA 15221-0882

Additional Titles by John W. Stanko

A Daily Dose of Proverbs

A Daily Taste of Proverbs

A String of Pearls

Changing the Way We Do Church

I Wrote This Book on Purpose

Live the Word Commentary: Acts

Live the Word Commentary: Mark

Live the Word Commentary: Matthew

Strictly Business

The Faith Files, Volume 1

The Faith Files, Volume 2

The Faith Files, Volume 3

The Leadership Walk

The Price of Leadership

Unlocking the Power of Your Creativity

Unlocking the Power of Your Productivity

Unlocking the Power of Your Purpose

Unlocking the Power of You

What Would Jesus Ask You Today?

Your Life Matters

Made in the USA
Middletown, DE
19 April 2019